Shoot to Thrill! The Life and Times of a Reality TV Cameraman.

by

Sean Michael Davis

Shoot to Thrill! The Life and Times of a Reality TV Cameraman.

Library of Congress Cataloging-in-Publication Data
Davis, Sean Michael -1968
Shoot to Thrill! Memoirs / by Sean Michael Davis

ISBN 978-0-578-49996-3

1. United States – Arts in Education – Non Fiction.

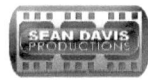

Dedication

This book is dedicated to my soul mate, Suzie, my son, Kasen, and all of my family and friends who have supported me through this crazy career! God bless you all ☺

Sean's book reads like a novel though it could well be a text book for all genres of film making. At the very least it should be at the top of every film school reading list. Be you a student or simply curious how movies are made, with this book comes the complete curriculum.   Be they features, documentaries, cooking shows and yes, action packed reality shows like "COPS", you'll be along for the ride with the people who produce them. Following his career from its beginning to today the reader learns as Sean learns and experience the feelings that come with the job. Excitement, exhaustion, satisfaction, frustration and fear to name a few. But like many if not most after more than twenty years on the job he still loves it. How is that possible? That's easy, it's also his hobby!
Bob Hite – News Channel 8 senior anchor (ret.)

Contents:

Athens, GA
Santa Claus, IN
Boston, MA
NY, NY Tampa, FL (when not to be an idiot!)
Boston, MA
Austin, TX
Payback Flatulence
Lost Items
Bed BugsFloral Park, NY
The Traveling Penis
Albany, NY (Winter Storm Stella)
Tweak Your Space
Antiques Roadshow
Fantastic Food
Docomo Koji Mochinaga
Mike Pence, Vice President

Some names have been changed to protect their identity, and it would have been impossible to get releases from everyone mentioned in this book. Others have remained the same, as they are happy to be a part of the experience.

This book does not have chapters, just memories, moments, and laughs.

Foreword

Just like most people I know, I have a "bucket list". I have been blessed over the years to be able to scratch many things off of that list, but as we grow older, we hopefully add more things to our list. When we stop adding we are no longer living. I have always wanted to write a book, and I started to write one about ten years ago on independent filmmaking, but of course I was side tracked as my career started to become very busy.

Another item on my list was to create a feature-length film. Something I had shot and put together myself, and after three years of working on it between paying jobs, I finally finished Skyway Down – A Permanent Solution to a Temporary Problem. Skyway Down is a film about people who have ended their lives by jumping off of the Sunshine Skyway Bridge located in Tampa, Florida. After watching a young lady jump off of the bridge to her death, I decided that topic was now going to be the next item on my bucket list. Skyway Down is a film that I am very proud of and won "Best Florida Film" in 2012 at the Sunscreen Film Festival.

After the film was finished, I started noticing all of this extra time I had on my hands and started thinking about writing my book again. This time, I thought I would write about my adventures working behind the scenes on the TV reality show COPS. This job had most definitely offered some very exciting and scary moments for me, and I thought this in and of itself would be a very interesting

6

book to write. As in most cases, life took over, and I never seemed to find the time to sit down and start writing memoirs about my time with COPS. Soon after that, my good friend and one of my soundmen during my time with Langley called me up and said, "Hey, I need you to sign this release, because I just finished my book about being behind the scenes of COPS and you are in the book." Well, so much for that idea!

Again, life gets in the way with all the little things we want to accomplish on our life's journey, and things like bills and mortgages affect our ability to work on some of our goals. Time has progressed in my career, and I have decided the best book to author will be a simple memoir of my life experiences in a wonderful business that I am so blessed to be a part of. The life and times, and crazy experiences, of being a cameraman in reality TV.

As with every person on the planet, there is always the "back story" and mine is interesting, and it's nice to archive the family lineage in this way. So I hope you enjoy reading this book as much as I have enjoyed writing it. The memories, the learning experiences, and the sometimes-painful lessons learned along the way.

The Early Daze
(yes, play on words)

My great grandfather, James Davis, was a stonemason and a sculptor born in 1870. For generations, his family had resided in a beautiful little coastal community called Swanage, Dorset, located along the southeastern coast of the United Kingdom.

At twenty-nine years of age, he married my great-grandmother, Susan Pierce Woolage. By 1907, they had three children, Edna, Walter and Willfred. Like so many others, they sought a better life in America. Eight years after their marriage, they boarded the S.S. Philadelphia and traveled from England to Buffalo in October 1907, where a job was offered in his field of stonemasonry. The Davis' had two more children in America, William (1913) and Beatrice (1917).

My grandfather, William James Davis went onto become an accomplished cereal chemist and business owner, and served as President of the New York Chemists Association. On a blind date, he met my grandmother, Virginia Olive Woeffel. At her young age, she was already an accomplished musician with a beautiful contralto voice. She had regular radio shows on WBEN, WGR, and WKBW in Buffalo, where she sang with a trio of girls known as the "Vocalettes." Beautiful on the outside and inside, Grandpa was smitten by Virginia, and they married in July of 1938. She was just twenty-two. After struggling with infertility issues for seven years, they conceived and gave birth to a ten-pound baby boy, my father James Kevin Davis. Dad was enamored with his mother's business of broadcasting, and at age fourteen he began his radio career on a suburban Buffalo radio station. It was his only career for the rest of his life, and even though he is now retired, he still does part time voice over work and also hosts an online radio station. The roots had been planted for a genetic lineage of arts and music.

My dad's extensive career in radio over the years allowed him to experience magical moments in radio, including announcing the Beatles, being part of the Motown explosion, and always having a career that was more fun than being an actual job. My dad was my first influence in filmmaking, when I was about six years old he brought home a camera from work. It was huge and must have weighed a couple hundred pounds! I remember making a rocket ship from paste, and we filmed it in the garage. It was so much fun to see the video playback after we shot it! Music has always been a huge part of my life as

—

well. As a child, I loved to draw and listen to music, and as I grew into my teenage years, I started playing the guitar.

I love the guitar and the piano. One of my other bucket list items will be to learn the piano as well. In my teenage years, I dabbled in bands, growing my hair long, wearing ridiculous clothes, and pretty much doing anything to try to look cool enough to possibly get laid! Sometimes it worked, most of the time it didn't.

The artistic side of me has always prevailed. School was not a "friend" to me as I never really made good grades. I slept through most of my classes, and did just enough to pass so I could graduate and find out what was next for me. My mom and dad divorced when I was young, and she remarried when I was around ten years old. My stepfather Richard Sweet had been in the military, he was a drill sergeant during the Korean War and was thinking about a military career for me as well. My senior year of high school I was pretty lost as far as college or career, I really had no focus, so I thought I would sign up for the Marines. My step dad was fine with this; I'm not sure if my mom was too keen on it, but since I really didn't have any idea of what else to do, I went ahead and talked to a recruiter and took my Physical and ASVAB exam. (Armed Services Aptitude Battery) Days before I was going to sign up, my father called me and offered an alternative to the Marines. "There is a music school in Orlando called Full Sail," he said, and he was offering me an education in the music engineering field. I was not sure what I should do, so I asked my stepdad about the offer. He said to me in his usual calm voice after thinking about my question, "Well… your love for music is obviously your gift, and your father is offering you an amazing opportunity, so why would you not take it?" So of course, I jumped on this opportunity and started Full Sail in 1987 after just barely graduating high school.

Full Sail was an amazing school developed by two men, John Phelps and Gary Jones. They had rented out a bunch of warehouses off of Douglas Avenue in Altamonte

Springs, Florida, and had organized labs and internships at the local recording studios. This was an amazing time for me in so many ways. My sister Renee was living in Orlando and going to school to be a flight attendant, so my dad agreed to have us rent a two-bedroom apartment and he would cover the rent. My sister Renee has always been, and will always be one of my best friends, so we made fantastic roommates! School had classes that were difficult for me, but I really wanted to learn the trade. So for the first time in my life, I actually applied myself and "hunkered down" and studied.

During this time, I met Lara Drum. She moved in with us after a while of dating, and Renee had started dating a young man named Johnny, who was also living in the apartment. So to say the least, we had a houseful. Mostly good times, Johnny worked at the Olive Garden, and he would frequently bring home free dinners! They also had a dog named Stoley who was an adorable white pooch. Some great times were had in this house full of laughter and love. Renee and Johnny wound up falling apart, and Renee left for her first flight attendant job, so now it was just Lara, me, Johnny and Stoley. Then eventually Johnny left, so we wound up renting the extra room to one of my Full Sail friends so we could have a couple extra bucks.

This was also around the time I had met Michael Knowlen. We met at a party, and he eventually became one of my very best friends. His girlfriend's name was Donnette, and they eventually married and had a son who is named after me, Sean Michael. I was honored to accept the responsibility of God Father for this beautiful child. Michael had a dream of becoming a movie director, and I had never even thought of this field as I was so enveloped in the music side of my life. We would all drive over to Tampa and spend the weekend at mom and dad's house sitting out on the porch until the late hours of the morning, me playing my guitar and Michael telling us about his new idea for a movie. They usually involved a dragon and some medieval hero.

Michael wound up signing up for the Marines and served in Desert Storm. In some ways this was a comfortable closure for me, since I did not go through with the military commitment I had intended on, Michael did it for me by becoming the Marine I had not.

My stepbrother Pete took a different path in business, and he worked several positions in his direction while I was finding my career. Pete became very successful creating his own water mitigation company. Unlike myself, Pete was always very studious and a straight A student most of the time, and very driven to be successful, which he now is. I am very proud of my brother.

Full Sail was a yearlong program and offered classes in so many areas of musical engineering. Some classes came easy to me, but some did not. I think I was able to comprehend the "hands on" type classes fairly well, but the "geeky" technical classes were more difficult for me. Classes like MIDI confused me, because I was never very computer savvy, and MIDI was most definitely a computer-based concept. MIDI stands for Musical Instrument Digital Interface, and basically it allows you to chain several electronic instruments together and allows them to talk to each other. For example, you could have three keyboards, a drum machine, and a couple of tone modules for the keyboards all connected to a sequencer. Then you could control them, change the sound of the keyboards or the drum machine, and record tracks on the sequencer. This basically allows you to become a one-man band, in a sense.

Awesome concept, and I had several rigs over the years, but I never really locked in on the idea of digitally chaining instruments together. Eventually, I realized in general it was easier for me to grab a guitar and just play. Full Sail had a couple of brand new technologies at their disposal. One was called the Synclavier, which consisted of a large keyboard-looking control panel, a huge rack hard drive called a Winchester Drive, and endless possibilities! This was an amazing piece of really expensive gear that would allow you to connect musical notes or sound effects to a time-code-based project. In one of my labs, I had a video that I needed to add sound to. It was a war film of fighter planes in the sky involved in a dogfight, which I would have to scroll frame by frame through the footage of the machine gun spinning. At the very first frame I would see a flash from the bullet, then I would have to enter the time code into the computer system as "in and out points", and then assign whatever gunshot sound I thought sounded best and move on to the next frame. I went frame by frame until I had done probably three hundred in and out points, as well as finding explosions and plane sounds. The frames were based on a time code called SMPTE which stood for Society of Motion Picture and Television Engineering. This was the universal time code everything in the United States is based off of, and was implemented from NASA. When it was all said and done, this forty-five second clip probably took me three days of lab time to finish, but it did look and sound pretty cool when it was done. This project would be my first real experience in video editing.

The other really cool thing they had just acquired was a mixer board called the SSL (Solid State Logic). Mixing consoles have been around for many years, but this was cool because the faders (volume level controls) had "Memory". This meant that as you are mixing the tracks of a song, the board would record your movements of the faders, and when you were finished, you could stand back away from the board and watch the faders all move up and down by themselves. This was so cool to watch, and it just made the recording studio even more awesome to me, as I was just so at home in this environment and could not wait for my next studio adventure.

Lara was working at a veterinary clinic, and her dream was to go to Vet school and become a Veterinarian. We would sit up at night in our apartment talking about our dreams of having a huge house that had a recording studio at one side and a vet/kennel facility at the other end, where she could do clinical field research from her own home lab. It's always so nice to have goals and dreams when you are young, and I really think goals and dreams are the fuel that keeps us moving forward. Include a little fate and some luck into that fuel, and that's what brings us to our final career decisions.

While I was attending Full Sail they only offered the Recording Engineering Program, but they would later start a film program that would allow the school to explode in the education industry! John and Gary were able to go from teaching out of rental units and shut down grocery store classrooms, to purchasing a city block campus and expanding their programs exponentially. Full Sail is probably the most high end and well-known school for film and audio production in the world now.

As the school year came to an end, I did my internship at a studio called Stark Lake Studios. It was a beautiful studio and owned by a really nice couple, but after my internship I was awakened to the reality that my school schedule was over. I now had to actually get a job and start my career. I worked several jobs, none of them music-related. Construction, washing dishes at a strip club, and finally I got a job at Video Production Center. VPC was basically a mom and pop editing facility that rented out booths with video decks in them. They also had a back room that, for its time, was a high-end video editing suite. The other part of the building consisted of racks and racks of VCRs all chained together where they duplicated VCR tapes. They had a monthly contract with a grocery store franchise, a church, and some mail order companies of old black and white films. My job was working the night shift and it sucked! I would load each tape deck with a tape, set bars and tone, hit record on each deck, then play on the master deck, and set a timer for the half hour or hour the show needed. Then after the recording had ended, I would remove each tape and insert it into a sleeve, and place them all in bins for the day crew to send out.

It did not take long for me to realize that at this pace, my goals and dreams would take years to accomplish, if ever. So I went back to Full Sail and talked to my old guidance counselor. I explained my predicament, and she offered me an opportunity. "There is a new TV show being shot over at the Universal Studios sound stage called Swamp Thing, and they are interviewing for a group of unpaid interns to work on the show. Why not go over and talk to them?"

Why not? What do I have to lose? So, I drove over to the Back Lot of Universal and walked into the BBK production office. I had a great conversation with Gina, a production coordinator, and she offered me the internship. Wow! What an opportunity! Lara was going to community college pretty close to Universal, so we rented an apartment closer to the sound stage, and I started my internship on Swamp Thing!

I can tell you now, this internship changed the course of my career goals forever! I no longer wanted to be an engineer or work in a recording studio. I became absolutely enveloped in every aspect of filmmaking! The first lesson I learned on day one of my internship driving into the back lot of Universal Studios, was the union problems. The union IATSE (International Alliance of Theatrical Stage Employee's) had pulled all of the crew from the show because of financial regulations. The production company was not paying union rates or providing union benefits, so they pulled the entire crew. The production company replaced them with non-union workers who were willing to work for a lesser rate.

All of the old crew was picketing at the gate, waving signs and flipping me off as I drove past them because they thought I was taking their job. They had no idea I was an intern working for free, and this was my first time watching and somehow being a part of a union confrontation. This is not really that uncommon, as this is what the union does. They try to maintain higher rates for their members, but sometimes that means those members are pulled from paying work.

This internship lasted a full season of thirteen episodes, and gave me the opportunity to work in many departments, such as camera, sound, grip, electric, and special effects.

I was immediately attracted to the camera department, but it was very technical, and I honestly had no real photography background. You would think the sound department would have been my go to, but actually I really clicked with the grip guys. Tommy Hinson was our Key/Dolly grip, and he really became like a big brother to me. I worked really hard during my time with Tommy. If you're reading this, and you already have a good understanding of the different departments in the film industry, you may already know that working as a grip is physically demanding. Thank God I was young and in good shape. I was really interested in all of the gadgets and gear, the different lights, and the stands, and what not. Most of the names of the lights and equipment were Greek to me, so Tommy gave me a Mathews catalog and told me to take it home and study it.

That was the best guidance and advice I could have ever been given just coming out of the gate! I did just that, I turned every page and read the names of the different stands, and offsets, and junior pins, and baby stands. Then I would show back up the next day and jump on the back of the truck and "noodle" with each piece of gear. Tommy and I have stayed friends to this day. If you ever need an amazing Key grip, call Tommy Hinson!

I have so many wonderful memories of this time during Swamp Thing, but one that will always stand out to me was when the production team needed to get some insert shots of the Swamp Thing, and the actor Dick Durrock was not available. His stand in was also booked on another gig, so they asked me because of my size to step in as the monster! Of course, I was thrilled, and so they led me to the special FX trailer, and first had me strip down to my underwear and then coated me with talcum powder. Then they placed all of the monster parts on me, starting with the legs, then the hips and chest, and then the arms. All of these monster parts were rubber with leaves and green algae looking stuff on them. The entire night I was standing next to the man-made swamp. As the cameras rolled, the director would tell me to "lean my hand into the swamp water", or "step into the water", or "walk down a swampy path". It was so much fun, and I was able to get a picture at the end of the night wearing this amazing costume so I would always be able to remember this great experience.

After the season ended, I was back to not having anything to do. Of course, I was working part time, digging "footers" for a new housing complex. Yes, this sucked, but the money was actually not bad because no one else wanted to grab a shovel and "git-r-done." My family did not have a lot of money, but we were rich in love growing up, and all of my siblings were taught a solid work ethic.

It didn't take too long before my first call came in from one of my contacts from BBK. They were coordinating a TV commercial with MC Hammer, and needed a Production Assistant. I can't even remember the day rate, but I was thrilled! At that time, Kentucky Fried Chicken had an ad campaign involving a fictitious town called Lake Edna. The concept for the one-day commercial was MC Hammer's tour bus breaks down in Lake Edna on their way to a show. When a little boy rides along on his bike and sees the broken-down bus, he rides over to KFC, gets a bucket of chicken, and rides back over to the bus offering the food to Hammer and his posse. This wonderful basket of chicken was so well received by the rap stars that they commenced to dance in the streets, and the world was good again. Well, almost.

What none of the cast or crew knew, was that the location they decided to shoot at was a street corner right next to the H.R.S. (Human Resources) building on a

Monday morning. Lines of people were building outside the front office, as these individuals were waiting to collect their food stamps. For them to see this gross display of wealth and money basically being thrown away was upsetting, to say the least.

As you may or may not know, a national commercial of this magnitude has a huge cost attached to it. It's not uncommon to spend $300,000 for a thirty second spot, so we had all of the good stuff set up. Catering trucks, craft service tents full of snacks and shrimp and steak tips, fancy cars, big trucks, expensive gear, etc.

To these locals, this was invasive and insulting. After we started shooting, we would have to cut because of sound issues. Meaning, the locals were yelling profanities at the crew. Of course, the Assistant Director went to us (the crew), telling us to go over and tell these angry individuals to please be quiet so the talent can say their lines. Yeah, that worked. NOT!!!! Somehow, the production company was able to get everything they needed, though I'm not sure how. As the day progressed, so did the anger from the local crowd. Toward the end of the day, the locals pushed down the barrier wall we had set up. One of the assistant producers came to me and told me, "You are no longer a production assistant, you are going to be a body guard! Get in front of Hammer, and don't let anyone touch him!"

The crowd was getting wild, and as the crew was trying to wrap up equipment, the tension was getting dicey. I ran over to Hammer and his posse and stood in front of him, pushing people out of his way and trying to yell with my best mean voice for them to get back. I really wanted to say, "You can't touch this!" but I thought that might get me in trouble. LOL. When the day was finished and the commercial was wrapped, Hammer and his posse were all able to get back on the bus, and they drove off the set to safety.

It was an adventure for sure, and I totally knew I wanted more of this crazy, fun excitement of the film business.

As time progressed, unfortunately I was not getting any more calls for jobs, and the phrase "out of sight, out of mind" became the case for me. Because the calls for work became fewer and fewer, I wound up taking a job at Circuit City installing car stereos. I worked there for a couple of years, and I did get a call from Tommy to work on G.I. Jane, but the timing wasn't good, and I had to turn it down. After a while, Lara and I moved to Gainesville so she could start her education at the University of Florida. Obviously, Gainesville is not a bustling town for the film industry, so I hung up my filmmaker's hat and went to work at a local dive shop. I really did enjoy the dive shop and became a scuba instructor. As the years went by, I pretty much forgot about my time in film and just kind of moved on. I spent a couple years at the dive shop teaching scuba and running trips to the Keys and West Palm, which honestly did not suck. After a while though, I did miss the studio environment, and applied for a job at a local radio station, Kiss 105.

The radio station was across the street from our apartment, and one day I just walked in to ask for a job. Doug Gillen, who owned the station, happened to be there that day and liked me, so he offered me a sales job. I had done sales in the past with Circuit City but never a radio sales job. I figured what the hell, my dad and grandma were in radio, so why not give it a shot? This change of career from scuba training to radio sales was such a wonderful transformation back to my creative side! I was able to be prolific again, with copy writing and music, and the whole environment of entertainment. I had a couple weeks of sales training with Doug, and my first day out on the road I was able to get a signed ad schedule! I got the client to sign because he was a scuba diver, and as we chatted, he noticed the dive plate on my car, and our conversation turned from radio advertising to scuba diving.

After an hour of "dive talk", he told me he would be happy to agree to the ad campaign, and not only signed the contract but gave me a check! This was a wonderful thing to bring back to the radio station on my first day of selling, and Doug was so happy for me. What I really learned from this experience that would help me in the future with filmmaking, is how to communicate, find people's emotions and needs, and make those needs become a reality.

The most important thing you can do in any sales position, no matter what you are selling, is to develop trust based on sincere concern for their business, and your ability to make their concerns less. If your client believes you can help them, they will allow you the opportunity based on the small amount of trust you have developed. If you are successful the first time, it can become a long-lasting relationship.

Doug and I spent the next couple of years working together while Lara was finishing school. When Lara was getting ready to graduate, my dad called me with the offer to take a radio sales job in Tampa. Doug was very understanding about my need to move, and helped me with all of his wonderful guidance and friendship. This would be a significantly larger sales market and would I be prepared for this. My job in Gainesville was honestly the most difficult job for me to ever leave, as Doug had become like a big brother to me. I trusted and loved him, so to leave would mean no support, a new environment, and surroundings that I was unfamiliar with. I knew this could either go well or go really bad for me.

Lara graduated and we moved to Tampa so I could take a job working for Clear Channel. My dad was working for Clear Channel at this time, and he was able to pull some strings to get me this job. Recording studios and crazy fun people again! This just made me miss the film industry even more. Honestly, I was bored with sales, and so I decided to try and get back in the film business. I had pretty much lost all of my contacts over the years. Tommy was in North Carolina, and I was not planning on relocating again.

I started working on anything I could for free, and started being a part of the local film groups. On my days off, I would get together with friends who had written shorts, and we would compile a handful of gear between us and shoot anything we could just for fun. There was a local group called the Tampa Film Network, and once a month we would all meet up. They would play three short films that had been shot, and then the filmmakers would come up and talk about their films. One guy had a web blog and he would rate the films. We started submitting our shorts, and were getting really good reviews from both the audience and the critics. So it was a good start to try and get my name back out in the local film community.

While working on local projects, I found a local gear rental shop called First Unit. First Unit is a Clearwater based rental house for grip and lighting equipment. The owners, Rick and Doug, were both very friendly, and were happy to let me be a part of the team, as long as I was willing to help out around the shop. As time progressed, I would spend as much time as I could working in the shop, loading trucks and fixing equipment. I spent quite a bit of time originally making Apple Boxes with my newfound friend, Kurt Koutz. Kurt is an amazing technician, who not only knows woodworking, but also grip and lighting. I later found out he is an Assistant Director with the union. These are the contacts you make while working in the industry. First Unit is owned by Rick Kalivoda and Doug Fenclaw, and they are both awesome dudes who know their stuff. Rick showed me several different types of lighting gear, as he is known as the best local lighting director in the industry, and I was able to work with Doug many times on set. During my time working at First Unit, I was able to meet so many of the local camera/director of photography people in the area, as they would come in to rent gear. One of my close friends was Gio Kozick, who worked at First Unit as the primary technician, and he is amazing. He knew every piece of gear in the shop, and he really did teach me quite a bit. Gio also helped me understand the grip trucks, and how they are loaded, and what needs to be used.

Local Beginnings

When Lara and I moved to St. Petersburg, Florida, one of the main reasons I contacted First Unit was because I had been told the best way to get into the business would be to make friends with all of the local filmmakers. What a better way to do that, than to see them face to face as they pick up gear? So, I offered to work for free on my days off, so I could start learning the ropes and meeting the local clientele.

I started with several projects they had been working on; Rick and Doug were in the process of making the new Apple Boxes for the three trucks they owned. First Unit has always been known for keeping all of their trucks and equipment in pristine condition, so it was common to see Rick pull all of the C Stands off the truck, and have the crew clean and oil them. Just for reference, one thing about this business is every piece of equipment has a name (usually more than one), and the sooner I could memorize them all, the better. Most of the names made sense, an Apple Box was called that because it is a simple square box used all the time, and looks similar to an apple crate. They come in four different sizes, and are named based on their size: full apple, half apple, quarter apple and then pancake. I'm assuming pancake was named that because it is flat and thin.

Apple boxes get beat up pretty quick, because they are used for just about everything, and get tossed around the set. My job was to brand each one with the First Unit logo, and then to clear coat the boxes. Kurt was making the boxes and assembling them, and then I would brand them in the press, and then apply the clear coat and set them out to dry. I would also help to load and unload trucks, and just about anything else we needed in the shop. I worked at the shop on and off for about two years, and eventually left Clear Channel so I could pursue this almost full time toward the second year. During this time, I became friends with so many local professionals, and started being given the opportunity to work on many local commercials. Todd Short, a local Key Grip, started bringing me on a lot of his jobs. He knew I was pretty green, but we became friends and he started teaching me a lot of the trade, similar to the way Tommy Hinson had during my internship.

During this time, I started working with groups on the forty eight hour film contests. These were hard, long hours, but so much fun. It was a way I could start shooting and directing on a small level. I met Cliff Gephardt while working on a local project. We were shooting in one of his buildings, and he told me about an idea he had for a TV pilot. It was about all the crazy things that have happened in his buddy's pawn shop over the years. I responded to Cliff, "If you're serious, then write it down." This was usually a good way to separate myself from all the people who "had a great idea for a film". Once you get into this industry, everyone and their brother has a great idea for a film, but they want you to do all of the work.

Cliff was different. He really is a go getter, and it showed. He purchased script writing software and started writing. When I read it, I could not stop laughing. I had never worked on a comedy, and was excited to shoot this one, so we became partners and started the process of making a show. Cliff rented an abandoned laundry mat and started converting it into a pawnshop. He built fake walls, got shelving from a closed down K Mart, and all of his friends started dropping off all of their junk. We had old computers that no longer worked, power tools, and fishing rods, and we got a couple of broken display cabinets and fixed them up. Within a month, we had a pawnshop called "Big Joe's Pawn Shop." Cliff had a local vinyl sign guy do all the front windows with signage, and it looked so real that people started coming by to pawn stuff. We had to put a sign on the front door that said "This building is not a real pawn shop, just a film location, do not enter." We would still get the occasional drunk, who would try to barge in while we were filming.

I had worked with an actor named Brett Rice on several small projects over the past year, and had become friends with him. One of my friends, Joey Reinhart, knew him, and we had done a short film called Autographs for French Fries. So when it became time to cast, Brett was my first thought, and he agreed to do it for $500 bucks, a hotel room, and a bottle of Crown Royal. We held casting calls at a local theater venue, and what a great experience. I met so many wonderfully talented people during the castings, and we assembled a fantastic cast. A local news anchor Bob Hite was very supportive of the film community. Bob even interviewed us, and put us on News Channel 8 supporting our endeavor.

We started principle photography on Pawnd, and shot for three long days. I directed the project, and a very talented shooter, Eric Curtis, was the DP/Shooter on the show. The experience was a blast, the editing came out great, and before long, we had a full twenty-two minute pilot. The show premiered at the Sunscreen Film Festival and took home "Best Florida Film." Then we submitted it to the Crystal Reel Awards annual competition, and took home several awards: Best Directing, Best TV Pilot, and Best cinematography. The most amazing part was when Cliff took it to the annual Pitch Pit in Las Vegas, and Comedy Central became very interested in the project.

Cliff and I had several conference calls with the network, and came very close to selling the show. Unfortunately, in the end they went with another show, but we were so close. The entire social response really helped put my name on the map as a strong independent filmmaker though, and phone calls started coming in again. Since I had started to work part time at First Unit, and was now in the clique of the people who were making a solid living in this industry, day jobs were starting to come in. A month or so later, Cliff and I partnered again for a forty eight hour film contest, and we brought in the same talented cast we had used in Pawnd, as well as some more actors. This time, we were able to use my friend Curtis Graham's studio for casting and writing. Curtis is an amazing DP and he was willing to offer his talents with the contest as well, as his equipment. First Unit also lent us a full grip and lighting truck, and several of the staff also became part of our team. By the time we finished, we counted about seventy cast and crew for our project. This film was called A Minute Too Late, and it did great as well. Best directing, Best cinematography and editing! The Forty-Eight hour film contests are a blast. The way to keep the teams honest, is during sign up they give you a genre (ours was murder mystery), specific names or words to be used in the script, as well as specific props or locations that need to be used. This way you cannot write an amazing script weeks beforehand. They are a lot of fun to be a part of, and always a great learning experience.

Lesson Learned

I have told you about my upbringing into this film world, but there has to be a start when you really learn your art.

Yes, I did some cool things, but they were on a personal level, not a professional level, and this was my first real life lesson.

So, after having all of these wonderful local people telling me how much they liked my films, and how amazing I was, I learned my first real lesson in humility in the professional world of cinematography. A friend of mine, Todd Thurgaland, who was a producer/shooter and also knew my dad, owned a company shooting training videos for law enforcement, and had recommended me to his friend to help him on a shoot in the panhandle. It was part of a shoot doing "behind the scenes" for a calendar company. I was to meet my client in Ocala, and then ride with him to the panhandle. For those of you who are not familiar with Florida, this is the upper west end of the state. Paul Pruwitt, my client, was a friendly man, and had just come off of a long shoot in Cuba and was obviously exhausted. Paul had been shooting amazing videos of Cuba way before we were allowed to travel there. My job was to be his camera assistant. I was so excited to be on this job, as I would be working with Paul and his camera, which at the time was so high tech and state of the art. It was the new Sony 900 Cine Alta, a tape-based camera that all of the large production companies were using. I met Paul and jumped in his car to make the seven-hour drive to the panhandle, and we were able to have a conversation about his trip in Cuba, and what he was shooting, and all of the amazing things he saw while he was there. While having this lengthy conversation, I told Paul about how awesome I was, and all of the amazing things I had done, and did I mention how awesome I was? LOL. So Paul, in his infinite wisdom, gave me the opportunity of a lifetime. Paul said, "You know what? I'm just going to let you shoot this because I am so tired!"

I was exhilarated! I'm going be the shooter on this high-end project? How cool am I? So, we checked into the hotel room, and while Paul was fast asleep, I got online and tried to learn everything I could about this camera that

I had never shot on before! I was trying to learn the color balance and the filters and the settings and everything else.

Day one arrives, and we start shooting. We start on the beach, shooting beautiful woman laying on kayaks, under beach umbrellas, and playing in the surf. I shot all day, shooting ladies on beach chairs and basking in the sun. We shot them that night in the bar, drinking shots and dancing with the band, and playing in the moonlight sand.

After the day was over and we were back at the hotel, Paul wanted to see the footage I had shot, and of course, and so did I. So, I put the first tape in the camera, hooked up a monitor, and did my first real play back of the day.

So let me put you in the hotel room with Paul and I. Paul is sitting at the desk across the room looking at the monitor, and I was standing five feet away excited to let him see the Emmy Award winning footage I had just shot. I was at that moment so sure he would be so happy with my footage, that he would now bring me on all his jobs. Maybe he would tell me to just shoot all of his gigs, and he'll just sit back and direct? Maybe he would want to make me his new partner so he can tell everyone that Sean Michael Davis is now his main shooter? Anything could happen! And it did!

The first thing I learned as soon as the footage started playing, is that since the viewfinder on this camera is in black and white, my color balance was dramatically wrong. The next thing I learned was that I SUCKED!!! My composition was horrible, my color balance was awful, and I was so shaky that it looked like an earthquake was happening most of the time! Some of the footage was ok and usable, but many shots were not good at all. The more I watched, the more I felt like I completely lost this day of shooting! Since the room was deadly silent, I was secretly praying and hoping that Paul was not noticing the same problems I was. Or even the very slight possibility that maybe he was okay with the footage? The room was so quiet, I could hear the clock on the wall slowly ticking away what felt like my life, and the sweat was now dripping off my forehead into my eyebrows, hopefully about to blind me so I did not have to keep watching! I was still truly trying to hang onto the hope that maybe, just maybe, I was just being over critical of my shooting. When I finally pulled myself out of my own hell for a moment to risk a glance at Paul, this clearly was not the case. Paul's face looked like he was watching a horror movie. What I saw was an open mouth, eyes wide-open, and a look that if he turned his head towards me, I am pretty sure would turn most mortals into stone! The first thought that came to mind was how quickly I could make this moment end. If I was to fake a heart attack, would that help? Maybe Paul would feel sorry for me having a heart attack, and not be so upset? Maybe he would feel bad for me going into an epileptic seizure, and just write off the day. All of these thoughts were racing through my mind, but that did not actually help resolve the current issue. What made this experience even more uncomfortable, was the person I had convinced how great I was, is now watching my footage in complete amazement, and not in a good way. I was not sure how he would handle this. Paul was a big guy, and when he finally came out of his apparent trance, was he going to pick my ass up and throw me off the balcony of our room? Were there any weapons within easy grasp that he could pick up and stab through my eye? I was just waiting for the profanity and finger pointing to start, and for him at the very least to start yelling "What the hell were you thinking?" at me. To add insult to injury, we were only about seven minutes into a thirty-three minute tape. How long this pain would go on was completely up to Paul. I totally wanted to walk over and hit stop on the playback deck, and come up with some witty way of defending myself, like "hey, the sand was uneven?" But instead, I just stood there and waited for him to stand up and beat me stupid. Actually, I wanted him to start beating me stupid at this point. I would have totally deserved it, as the truth is, I oversold my capabilities based on arrogance. I had shot some great stuff prior, and it's not like this was my first time shooting, but I did not pay as much attention to detail as I should, and clearly got lost in the moment of just shooting.

Paul was clearly beside himself, because he thought I was this amazing shooter, and what he saw was not fantastic. We lost a good part of the day because I was the shooter.

The worst part was his reaction. I expected to be cursed at, beaten, or at the very least shanked, but Paul just looked at me like a disappointed father and said almost nothing. Just like your dad does when you really screw up! To me it was so much worse than getting yelled at, and yet the tape still played. Oh, please God, not the silent judgment, was it too late to fake that heart attack?

To be truly candid, Paul could not have been more kind and understanding about the day. He basically said, well that wasn't great and now we have to fix it. I didn't get a lot of sleep that night of course, but Paul took the camera over and shot the rest of the show while I just sat there as a camera assistant, and tried to get through the day doing what I was originally hired to do, and be as helpful to him as I could. I realized on this job that I didn't know as much as I thought, and I sure did learn from it! Paul did fix it, and reshot some of the beach scenes we needed, and did wind up getting what he needed for the show. Paul and I are great friends now, and to this day we still laugh about this experience, but mostly we talk about all the cool new gear that has been coming out.

As I continued to work locally, I was also introduced to HSN, the Home Shopping Network. HSN is located in Clearwater, and is a massive production facility with several stages and tons of equipment and employees. They are a twenty-four hour, three hundred and sixty-five day a year live broadcast facility, specializing in the sale of products. Between HSN and First Unit, I was able to start working enough each month to focus on my career a hundred percent, and I was thrilled! This was also about the time I met Bill Mills. Bill is an amazing Director of

Photography, who has won several Emmys for his work. Bill has a local production company and specializes in outdoor/underwater type shoots. He is a great lighting director and hand held operator. Bill started hiring me first as a grip, and then he started hiring me as his AC (Assistant Camera).

As time progressed, Bill and I worked on several projects together, and still do. We went to San Diego together and shot a Marine training video, and we have worked on several industrial type videos together, as well as a TV series with Emeril Lagasse.

Bill has mentored me through the majority of my shooting career, and he has become an amazing friend. Cheers, Bill.

Curtis Graham was another mentor figure during the early days of my career. Curtis is also an amazing cinematographer who started as a photographer. Curtis's dad owned a photography store in downtown St. Pete, and Curtis developed his dad's talent for composition and lighting. Curtis partnered with a friend and opened up his own studio called Indie Films. I would spend time at Indie Studios when I was not working, cleaning equipment, painting the CYC wall, and just hanging out. CYC stands for Cyclorama and is the rounded wall we shoot against. Curtis would hire me when he would get jobs, and several times I would drive his grip truck, which was probably one of the largest trucks I had ever driven. It was like a semi-truck full of grip gear that he had acquired over time. Curtis would also direct low budget features, and this also helped put me behind the camera more often than the grip truck. Curtis was getting tired of shooting and directing, so he started hiring me as his operator.

If there is any part of this book that I would want ANY aspiring filmmaker to read, it would be this part! Don't be afraid to work hard, make friends, work even harder, and be humble. Trust me, none of these people took me under their wing because I was a super duper camera guy. They took me under their wing because I was humble, willing to learn anything they were willing to teach me, and thankful for every minute they were willing to spend with me. Rule number one: Leave your ego at the door! Just because you graduated from film school, does NOT mean you are the next best filmmaker. You very well may be, but it's going to come from mileage in the field, not from a degree.

Starting My Career

In the ole-days, I remember when I was first starting out working nights and days off at First Unit, cleaning and loading trucks, I would occasionally get called out on a job that still required film. For the newcomers and film students, film is a dinosaur of sorts. When I was not on other jobs, occasionally I would get hired to work a show, usually with Curtis or Bill, and it would be a film job. Curtis still owned an ARRI 35mm film camera, and he would use this when he had certain commercials, usually food jobs for restaurants or such. Film looks so pretty, and has such an amazing depth of field and color. The new industry has really done a nice job replicating this look, but for me, nothing digital will ever have the warmth and feel of film. I remember doing several commercial jobs with Curtis using his ARRI 35, which I remember the motor was so loud. We would only use it for MOS shots of food. MOS means "without sound", it was a German term coined a long time ago from a famous director who called it "Mit Out Sound". Newer cinematographers state this acronym stands for Magnetic Operating Strip, which is a technical term also for older cameras, but who really knows? That was fifty years ago! Regardless, it was a loud friggin' camera, but it was beautiful, and I fell in love with it and so wanted one myself!

I remember working on a low-budget film with Curtis, and I had purchased a small box truck, and had built a dark room in the front of the box. I had seen these trucks in the past in feature film camera departments, so I bought a truck locally for three grand, and shelved it out and built the dark room in hopes that I could rent it on films. Curtis had just landed a job on a low budget Christian feature film, and offered me a day rate to include my truck. My position was to be a 2nd AC (camera helper), as well as the film loader on the job since I had the dark room. Truth be told, I had never loaded film on a job, and was pretty much clueless as to how to do this, but I took the position and Googled how to load film.

Curtis had planned on shooting this on the Red camera, which was a new digital camera, but it was not ready yet. So he decided to shoot on ARRI super 16mm cameras, which are beautiful film cameras, but it's film and requires a lot more work. That's why he hired me to be the 2nd AC/film loader. I learned the trade of a loader while doing the job; I had a big black zipper tent that I could place the film magazines (the upper part of the camera that held the film) in, and simply by feel would open up the mag and place it in a separate canister as well as tape it shut, then reload fresh film into the mag and give it back to the crew to use again. All of this had to be done by feel, as no light can enter the bag, or the film will become over exposed and ruined. I would then label the used film canister, and create a film report for the transfer with all of the camera information, regarding settings and exposure and such.

Interestingly enough, I never once used the darkroom I had built. The only time it was used was when the grips would sneak in and smoke pot during the day. Shooting film was way more complex than today's system of shooting everything digitally. Two major companies, Fuji and Kodak, made film. Kodak was the leading manufacturer of film, but Fuji also had nice film. They would constantly compete on pricing, so you would just buy it from whoever would sell it the cheapest. Film comes in two stocks, Tungsten and Daylight. They would have a number based on the speed and emulsion, and then be followed by a "T" or a "D" to let you know what type of film it was. During the day outside, you would use the D film. At night or indoor, you would use the T stock. It also came in different size loads: 100, 200, 400, 800, and 1000 feet. The standard was 400 feet, and this would give you approximately eleven minutes of shoot time. One day when we had a bunch of interns working, I remembered one of them coming up to the back of the truck while I was in the middle of this process to ask me what I was doing. I remember being so confident, I was the 2nd AC film loader! I had a very important job! I told them about how important my position was, and how critical what I did for the show was, and "Look, if I accidently open this bag up before it's ready then…" Holy Shit! I just did! I just opened the bag up before I had closed the can. I just "flashed the mag." That means I just let light in and over exposed the entire magazine of film. Eleven minutes of film destroyed! Totally my fault for being arrogant. Holy crap! Of course, I yelled at the intern who ran away, and then I had to deal with my situation. I had a full mag of exposed film! Think of the cost of eleven minutes of shot film. That could possibly be an hour of actual time with film crew, jib shots, push ins, perfect acting scenes, best performances ever. What was I going to do? I just screwed up possibly a big part of a day. Locations, crew, lighting, permits, etc. My heart was racing, but I had to do the right thing. Yes, I could say nothing, and they would find out later in post, and then scream and yell and never hire me again.

Or, I could own it now and eat my crow. So, that's what I did. I went to the AP (Associate Producer) and told him I just flashed a mag. He went to the director, and told him we just lost 11 minutes of footage. You could have heard a pin drop. The director then asked, "What were we shooting?" The AP told him it was the crane shot of the family walking into the house, and the close-ups of the wife opening the door.

His response was "Well…she sucked, and I want a different girl anyway for that part, so let's reshoot it next week." OMG! Really? How lucky was I?

Moral of this story, deal with your situation and be accountable. Without a doubt, honesty is always the best policy.

Another situation I will never forget, was a day we were shooting at the Clearwater courthouse, and after we wrapped for the day, I was loading my camera truck. One of the agreements I had made with Curtis to work on the film, was that I would also pull the generator behind my truck. Curtis had paid to have a hitch welded to the back of my truck so it could pull the generator, which would power all of our equipment so we would not trip any breakers in the locations we would be shooting at. It's very common on larger scale films and commercials to use a large generator. We had a bunch of interns working with us on this film, and one of them had hitched the generator back up to my truck for the drive back to the studio. It was getting late, and already dark by the time we wrapped that evening, so after I loaded all of my gear into the truck, I lowered the back door and climbed into the truck for the drive back to St. Pete. As I pulled out of the courthouse parking lot and into the street, I heard the loudest bang I think I had ever heard, opposed to a gunshot! Then there was a strong jerk motion against the truck, like something was pulling against it. I put the truck in park, and climbed out to see the generator completely unhitched and on the ground, with just the safety chains still attached to the truck. The generator itself was now resting on the road. This generator probably weighed a couple thousand pounds, so there was no way in hell I could physically lift it up and set it back on the truck hitch. What made this situation worse was that my truck, and the unhitched thousand-pound generator, was now blocking all of the oncoming traffic on the main road! After saying out loud just about every profanity I could think of, most of which would probably make a sailor cringe, I then grabbed my cell phone and called Rod Brandenburg, who was working with us and had just left minutes before I had. Rod was a great technician, and I knew he would be able to help me get this generator hitched back up quickly, if I could reach him before he got on the long bridge back to Tampa. Rod answered, and I'm pretty sure at first, he had no idea who was on the other end of the phone, as I must have sounded like a thirteen year-old girl screaming like someone had just stolen her iPad! Once Rod was able to get me to regain some form of composure, his first question was "Is anyone hurt?" I said no of course, and then he said, "Relax, I am turning around and will be their shortly, and we will get this fixed." Rod was always so calm, and I knew this would be ok. But now I was starting to see police car lights flashing, as the local law enforcement was now having to redirect traffic, since I was blocking the entire north bound lane. A stranger came up out of the blue, and said he would help me get this hitched back up, and pulled a jack out of the back of his truck bed. He had me back my truck up a couple of inches, and he placed the jack under the generator hitch and lifted it up, so I could back the truck hitch ball back under the generator receiver. We lowered the generator back onto the hitch, and this time we locked it so it was secure. Before I could thank this guy, he was off. As I was securing the cables, a police officer then walked up, and asked me to move the truck out of the road and park in the gas station across the street. I did this assuming he would have to get some information to fill out a report, and then I would be on my way. Not so much! Once I pulled the truck across the street so traffic could now move again, the officer first asked me the whereabouts of the other individual who was helping me. I responded, "I'm not sure. He just left." The officer then informed me that while running his plate, there was a warrant for his arrest!

Oh wow! "That sucks," I said. "Sorry for all of the inconvenience, but I am just going to get on the road." He smiled and said, "No, please turn around, because there is also a warrant for your arrest." What? Are you kidding me? Apparently not, because the officer handcuffed me and placed me in the back of his squad car. By this time, Rod had showed up and was just as confused as I was. So I told him through the police car window, "Not sure exactly what is going on, but I may not be at work tomorrow." Rod left because there was nothing he could do, and I was just hanging out in the back of this police car, handcuffed for what seemed like hours. Eventually, the officer climbed back into his car, and I asked him what was going on. His reply was you will find out when we get to the station. I pleaded to see the warrant, and he reluctantly pulled up his computer to show me the warrant. When the photo of the driver in question came up, it was clearly not me! He was Hispanic, and did not look a thing like me. I told the officer, "That's not me! Who is that?" Once he looked at the photo, and then over at me, he realized this was a mistake. He had run the plate of the truck, but had never really looked at the photo, and just assumed I had a warrant for my arrest. I get he was just doing his job, but I was totally freaking out! He opened his car door, and then the rear door, to help me out and removed the cuffs. He told me to go to the clerk's office and get this fixed, and then offered to drive me back over to my truck, but I told him I had spent enough time in the back of his car and would just walk to my truck. I did just that, and finally did drive home, but what a crazy adventure that night had become! If I had only had a crystal ball, I would have been able to see that, in the future, I would be spending a whole lot more time in a cop car!

It was only a week or so later while we were shooting in Orlando, that I remember someone coming up and telling me the news. Rod had just received a call from his doctor that his test results came back, and he had been diagnosed with cancer. Rod and Curtis were best of friends, and when they were not shooting films, Rod was a boat captain and owned a charter boat. Curtis would go out on Rod's boat on his days off to spear fish. Today was not a great day on set, as Rod had just been informed of his illness. I remember watching from around the corner when the director, the producer, Rod, and Curtis all formed a circle and prayed. Rod then went home to be with his family. Rod lost his fight with cancer a couple of years later. Rest in peace, my friend.

After this film ended, I still had a romance with the old film cameras that were quickly becoming dinosaurs. They were becoming cheaper to buy on eBay, and so I bought a CP16, a dinosaur for sure! They were used in the 70's for news programs and shows. I never actually shot a second of film on it, but used it for training. I ran mags through it with exposed film, unloaded mags in the bag, reloaded it, and ran it again and again, just to get comfortable with the system. But never again would I use this system as a paying job. Curtis bought the Red Camera, which was totally digital, and I had to learn that. Bill bought a digital camera, A Panasonic 3700 P2 camera, and both were hard drive based cameras. Everything was going digital.

Assistant Camera

As I started working with Curtis and Bill, one of the positions I started doing more frequently was the Assistant Camera position. Bill and Curtis both knew I was pretty familiar with their equipment, so instead of being part of the grip department, I started assembling their cameras and setting everything up before a shoot, so they could just get behind the camera. I really enjoyed doing this, as I learned more and more about each camera they were using. Since the basics never really change, it became easy for me to assume the position and prep the camera for each shoot. My job was to unpack the camera or cameras, and set them up on a tripod, or slider dolly, or whatever mounting system the shot required. Sometimes we were on a dolly on track called a Fisher or Chapman, and these were basically large rolling chairs with a camera mount that would be able to raise or lower at whatever speed was required.

Sometimes these systems would just roll across the floor, other times the grips would set up sticks of track (similar to a railroad track) as long as needed. The track comes in four foot or eight-foot sections, and you can make the run as long as you need. This does become a bit complex, if say you are outside in the woods, and need to place sixteen feet of track across a hillside. You would need a lot of base support, usually apple boxes, and then use a bunch of small wood wedges to level the track and make it secure enough to handle a significant amount of weight. The dolly itself weighs from 150 pounds up to 500 pounds, plus the cameraman riding it, and sometimes even the AC, as they may need to operate the focus. So you could really be looking at close to 800 pounds riding on this track.

Most of the time it was much more simple setups, like a camera on a tripod. Usually we had a bunch of different lenses, and each lens was called a "prime" lens, meaning it had a specific focal point. It was common to have a case of about six lenses, starting from a very wide lens, like a 28mm, up to a "long lens", like a 135mm. The higher the number of the lens, means the farther in it would "push in" on the subject. So, a 35mm would be a wide lens offering a view of a room, and the longer lens would be a much tighter shot of the individual in the room, like a head and shoulders shot. So, you would start your first take on a wide shot all the way through the dialogue, and then change lenses to push in on the person or persons talking, so you had different sizes of shots to edit. You see this on every TV show or movie you watch. This is also why it takes so many hours just to shoot a small scene of dialogue. Not just because the actors have to hit their lines perfectly, but they have to do this many times at many different focal lengths, so the editor has plenty of shots to put together.

A kit of lenses would usually have a 24mm, a 35mm, a 50mm, a 85mm, a 105mm, and a 135mm. This way, you would have many options to use for the scene. As an AC, I would set up the camera and usually start with a 50mm lens, so the Director can look at the shot and then fine tune. The other part of being an AC, is after the gear is set up, balanced, and ready to go, I would then have to pull focus. Pulling focus is an art in itself, and is not easy to do. As the talent walks up to the camera, or walks across the room, the focal length changes, and my job would be to roll the focus ring of the lens to match the distance of the person we are shooting. If the person was far away, say 20 feet, then I would make sure the focal length was the same. As they walk closer to the camera and then stop 5 feet away, I would need to roll the focus ring from 20 feet to 5 feet, but be mindful to make sure I was accurate in the distance during the walk forward. So, if they started at 20 feet and slowly started to walk towards the camera, they may stop at 12 feet to look away and deliver a line, then continue the walk until they got to the 5-foot ending. I would place tape marks on the ground so they knew where to land, as well as helping me with my focal marks during the walk.

Sometimes this is really easy to match, other times it can be very difficult. For example, Bill and I did a job for ESPN, and we were shooting high speed (very slow motion). This requires a special camera system called a Phantom, and it shoots around 1400 frames per second. A normal camera shoots an average of 30 frames a second, so when you play back a high-speed camera you can see every inch very slowly as they are running towards you. If it is not exactly perfect on every frame with focus, you get

30 seconds of blurry out of focus shots, before you require solid focus again! These jobs are when my position becomes a bit stressful, as it can be really hard to stay on perfect track every shot for a 10-hour day. Fortunately for me, this was a successful day, and everyone was very pleased with my focus pulling, and we made an amazing commercial. Other times however, if you do not hit your focal marks, you get to see a lot of out of focus blurry moments that last a long time during playback.

Another part of the job is to place a matte box on the front of the camera lens, and this allows you to place glass filters in front of the lens. Sometimes it's for effect, like a mist filter making the shot look soft and lovely, or sometimes it is to add a polarizer or neutral density filter in front of the lens. These work great for shooting through glass or cutting down extremely bright light, such as a driving day shot on a nice summer day. The effect filters go back to the early days of filming when they wanted the damsel to look heavenly, so they would either place pantyhose in front of the lens, or sometimes they would even rub Vaseline on the lens itself, to give the image a glossy effect. Just some fun Film Noir.

I still AC for Bill and Curtis from time to time, and I still enjoy it just as much today as I did back in the early days. The only difference is in the early days it was actual film cameras, and now it is very high-tech digital systems shooting 6 or even 8K.

To explain this as simply as I can, high definition TV is roughly 1080 lines of resolution, and this looks fantastic! Several years ago, this was the newest technology. High definition TV was all the rage. Now as I am writing this, we can shoot in 4, 6, or even 8 thousand lines of resolution. The main benefit of this technology is the editors can now push in on a shot, or completely re-adjust the framing, without losing any quality of the footage.

The new industry is a binary format. These formats utilize hard drives and a new crewmember, what we call a

DIT or Digital Information Technician. This would be the new crewmember on every set. The guy sitting at a desk on set transferring hard drives into the computer, as opposed to film loaders labeling film reels. Same concept, just new technology.

The young computer generation had overtaken the seasoned film crew at this point. It was inevitable, but sad to see, as many of my friends left their film careers because of the new younger techno kids. This is life, and this is growth, as the sad end to film has also introduced a wonderful new technology in filmmaking. Using a new digital format allows us to do so many great, new things with our footage.

COPS

In July of 2007, I received a call from someone I had never spoken with before. His name was Jimmy Langley, and Jimmy was part of the Langley family, not Langley, Virginia (Quantico), but Langley Productions. John Langley was the creator of a very well-known show called COPS. Jimmy, his nephew, was in Tampa working on a show, and one of his camera operators had quit. Jimmy was looking for a new shooter for the next venue, and remembered that one of his past sound guys lived in Tampa. So he called him, and asked him if he knew of anyone he could hire for this venue. The sound guy's name was Rob, and he had worked with the COPS film crew for many years. He knew the show, and also understood that this was not your normal production. It is real, and can be sad, scary, crazy, dangerous, and sometimes mentally exhausting. Rob had worked with me in the past, and he knew I had shot some crazy stuff, so he recommended me to Jimmy.

Jimmy asked me to meet with him in Tampa and discuss this possible opportunity, and I was excited to meet with him. While driving to his hotel room, I was prepared. I had a DVD of my demo reel, I had a professional resume to show, and I honestly thought a nice gig in Tampa shooting COPS would be amazing for my career.

Lara had recently given birth to our son, Kasen, and I really felt this opportunity could help us financially. So I was excited to meet with Jimmy, and try to get on this gig. I pulled up to the hotel, walked in, and took the elevator up to Jimmy's room.

Jimmy and I talked, and he asked me about my camera experience, and I told him all of the fun things I had shot and done. I handed over my package with my nice DVD and resume, and he pushed it immediately over to his side. He never even glanced at it. He looked at me and said, "This job is not like any job you have ever shot, it's totally different. You have to be professional, and appeal to the police, you have to get them to trust you. You also have to be able to deal with intense situations and not fold under pressure." I would fully realize later exactly what Jimmy was trying to tell me, but it would take some time, and some rough situations, before I would totally comprehend this message. After Jimmy finished explaining the job, he asked if I wanted it? I am a firearm enthusiast, and would like to say I know a lot more than most people, because of my years shooting guns and researching the art. Honestly, once we started our dialogue, we talked more about guns than my experience. Jimmy is also a gun enthusiast, and I think that's why he offered me the job. He knew most cops are also into firearms, and this would be a good common denominator to help me get their trust. Any responsible gun owner knows the level of respect one has to have towards firearms, and I also believe the cops would appreciate knowing I was safe and respectful of the weapons around us.

I told him I would like to shoot for the show, and would be excited given this amazing opportunity. Then Jimmy said, "Great! You will start next week in Seattle, Washington. It's a two month long show." Holy shit! Seattle? Two months? Leave next week? That was not part of my plan, as I had not intended on leaving Florida. I thought I would be shooting in Tampa. This was all a big surprise that I had to think about. I told Jimmy I would have to discuss this with my wife before I would be able to commit. Jimmy understood, but told me, "Well, just let me know tomorrow, because I have to hire someone immediately."

Wow! That was a whole lot of stuff to think about during that drive home. When I got home, I made sure the wine was chilled and dinner was ready, so Lara and I could have this conversation. Lara came home, we discussed it, and she agreed that this was an amazing show, and it could be helpful for my future and my resume. It could also help us pay some bills. So, I called Jimmy the next day and told him I wanted the gig. I can only imagine now how many other cameramen made the same decision, having no idea what they were actually committing to.

Jimmy told me I would hear from production in the next couple of days with my flight and hotel information. I did get an email a couple of days later, while my emotions were reeling with anticipation and nervousness. I flew to Seattle a week later, and landed, got my rental car, and drove to my hotel. A group of other shooters and sound guys showed up during the day, and we all met in a hotel room that I would learn was to be the office for the crew. If we had three teams, then we would each get our own room, and then another room that all of the cameras and gear would be delivered to. We would also set up a video station for reviewing tapes, as well a place to meet when needed.

I unpacked, and called Lara to check on her and Kasen. I was kind of nervous, because I really had never been this far away from home. Seattle! Holy cow! That's a long way away from St. Pete, for sure. Hell, across the country. I was just now meeting the other guys, and introducing myself to them. I tried to be professional and polite, but I could tell they all looked at me and probably giggled inside, knowing that I would possibly last a month or two. These guys had all shot for the show for many years, they had seen camera guys come and go all the time. One of them had been with the show since the beginning, and he had seen it all. Tragedy, sorrow, pain, agony, grief, suicide, murder, decapitations, hangings, you name it. This show really did put you in the front seat of reality TV!

All of them were friendly and accepting of me. They knew they were short a cameraman, which frequently happens on this show, and wanted to start this venue fresh. Hopefully, I would make it the eight weeks. If not, I'm sure Jimmy would find someone else, as everyone wants to shoot for COPS primetime, Saturday night on FOX!

I had so many emotions going on that first night in the hotel room, but although I did not know it, this was to be an incredible part of my life and my future.

Bad Boys! Bad Boys!

King County, Seattle, WA 10-17-2007

My very first COPS venue. Let me tell you, I was excited, nervous, scared, and confused all wrapped up in a six foot three, 230-pound package. This was the first full time gig away from home for an extended period of time. Two months at each venue, and I could not be farther across the United States from home! I checked into my hotel room after picking up the rental car, and went to the office to get my gear. All of the gear is Fed Ex'ed in from California and delivered to that room. The gear is checked in by each crewmember, either camera gear or sound gear, and another case has viewing equipment like an HD DVD deck, monitor, speaker, and a small mixing board that are all set up on the desk, so each night after work we can go in and insert our disk(s) and watch the footage. If a story was shot, or what we perceived to be a story, then we would log the footage in. We would take each release we had signed, and scroll through the footage to find the very first time that individual was filmed. Then we would write the time code down, as well as what they were wearing or any discernible markings like hats, tattoos, or clothing, so the editor would know that person's name, and could relate the release to them.

The way the show works is simple; we can shoot anything we want, as long as it is on public property. If the show is good, or we think it might possibly become a show, then we ask the individuals on camera to sign a release. A release is a legal document signed by the person filmed, allowing the production company to use this footage any way they wish. This authorizes them to use the footage for television broadcast, as well as any images they would want to use to promote the show. Getting a release signed is the tricky part, of course, as most people do not want to authorize this, or see themselves on TV being arrested. If everyone filmed that evening signs, then we overnight the disks and release forms back to Los Angeles, and then go on to our next night of shooting. On a busy night, it is not uncommon to get two or even three possible stories. The stories are then categorized as A, B, or C stories. A stories are car chases, foot pursuits, or fights. B stories can be high-adrenaline pieces, or interesting dynamic shows, like guns, drugs, K9 stories, etc. And C stories are ones that just have an interesting element that is not boring, or just a simple arrest.

Our crew is very small, consisting of a camera operator/field producer and a sound operator. Just two crew per car, as the camera and sound gear are wireless, since we may have to run and do not want to be slowed down by a tethered system.

Tethered means connected. Usually, when a cameraman and soundman are shooting, they are connected with a cable so the audio is clean and crisp. In this case, we are wireless, allowing us to separate from each other, and as long as we are remotely close, the audio is still good. If we get too far apart because we are chasing someone, then at least we still have the camera microphone to capture audio until the soundman can catch up.

The first night, I was able to meet the whole crew, which consisted of three teams that were scheduled to be in the Washington area. Langley had other teams in other states at the same time, as well. My sound guy's name was Mark, a tall, thin man with a big smile. He immediately made me feel at ease. The other team consisted of Richie Foreman and Steve Keiger, both veterans to the Langley show. I cannot remember the third team, but I remember they were all very nice. We played basketball during the day before we went to work, and then drank beers after filming each night to wind down.

The first couple of weeks were a blur to me, as I was trying to learn the ropes of shooting the show. Jumping out of the car quickly, keeping good focus as everything was moving so fast, and keeping good color balance as the shift turned from day, to twilight, to pitch black midnight. The cameras were Sony XDcam systems with a super wide lens. The XDcam means the media you record on is basically a Blue-ray disk called an XD disk. The camera is a full-size pig that weighs about thirty-seven pounds fully loaded, and is a bitch to run with, which I found out very quickly into my first venue. To say the least, this was a major learning curve for me. My footage still needed some work, as it was shaky from running, and the transition from running to handheld still needed some finesse. The trick I was learning about running with the camera, was when you left the car and went up to the vehicle or situation, you are filming with the camera on your shoulder. If for any reason the perp decides to make a run for it, you have to grab the top handle of the camera, and as you start running, lower the camera out to your side and down to the ground as far as your arm will go. This allows you to run, but keep the camera as steady as you can while running full sprint. Then when the chase ends, you lift the camera back up to your shoulder and continue filming. The trick is to keep this entire process as steady as you can. Mark had to leave two weeks into the venue for family reasons, so he was replaced with Hank Barr, a veteran to the show who basically started it so many years ago. Hank worked with John Langley on Geraldo Rivera's show in the early days, and when John Langley came up with the idea for the show COPS, he employed Hank to be the sound guy.

The idea for COPS came into fruition through a series of events. Back in 1986, Tribune Broadcasting had ordered five 2-hour live broadcasts for FOX, and Geraldo Rivera was signed as the host for the first of the five episodes. This one was for a show called Al Capone's Vault, which was located in an old hotel in Chicago. Nothing was found in the hotel, and when the camera crew and Geraldo went down to the basement, a dusty and dirty empty wine bottle was found. This was all they found in the vault, and it's tough to make a two-hour live broadcast compelling with just a dusty bottle. Malcolm Barbour and John Langley produced all five of these live broadcasts. One of these was called American Vice, and it was a documentary of the nation's new epidemic of illicit drug sales and use. The numbers were so great, that that a series was proposed by Barbour and Langley to Fox. Barry Diller, who at the time was head of Fox, insisted that a narrator/host be in the car with the crew.

The host (Geraldo) would have a wireless camera on him, but the camera and sound guy were connected with a cable, so you can imagine this would get hairy from time to time when they had to move quick! John and Malcolm were not keen on having a narrator, because a couple of times Geraldo had to leave for other contractual events. When he would have to leave, they found it was just easier to put microphones on the cops, and let them lead the viewer through the raid, or whatever they were filming that day. This worked out really well, and more importantly, it put the viewer in the front seat of the squad car! Hank had mentioned to John how effective it was just putting the mic on the officer, but John had already realized this, and had a plan in the back of his head to pitch this idea next. John's original idea was to call the show "Street Beat", and by 1987, they were in pre production of the first test episode. At the same time, a writers strike hit Hollywood, and this literally kicked COPS into the Fox schedule.

COPS, as it would be called, would run for many years to come, being the number one true reality show for a long time. In 1994, they went from a half hour show, to two half hour shows back to back, because the audience demanded it. As I am writing this, COPS is still currently filming, however Fox released the show and Spike TV picked up the series.

Hank is a wonderful man who truly helped me get through the rest of that first venue by offering his years of guidance and expertise. Hank would later write a book called The Jump Out Boys, which was about his years on COPS. Rich was also very helpful, and spent a lot of time working with me not only on the technical side of the camera, but also on the finesse of shooting the show in regards to being super steady and not shaky. A great lesson Rich taught me was to "dance on the balls of your toes". Lift your heels off the ground, and just move around on the bottom of your toes, this makes for a much smoother movement of your body. Kind of like having shock absorbers in your calves.

Two weeks into our venue, Jimmy showed up at the hotel to meet with the sheriff and the police department, as well as to spend time with the crew. Jimmy is a very matter of fact person. At first, I found him very intimidating, as he would review my footage, tell me all the things I was doing wrong, and then end with "If you can't shoot the show, you will be going home." I heard this many times from Jimmy, but in his defense, time is money and he needs good capable shooters, not just adrenaline junkies. Jimmy has seen cameramen come and go all the time, as this show is like no other show ever. It definitely has its own style, as well as a high level of difficulty, not just shooting it, but also being able to cope with some pretty intense and sometimes sad situations.

As a crew, we are placed on every high priority call all night long, so you have to learn very quickly to be safe and levelheaded all the time. Over time, Jimmy turned out to be a great friend, who I still stay in touch with. That first venue was difficult for me to get stories, so I was close to the chopping block, but I was on the phone quite a bit with Doug, the lead editor of post-production. He liked what I was shooting, so he decided to keep me for another venue to see if I would continue to improve. Jimmy replaced my sound guy, Hank, with another seasoned soundman, Robbie Stephens. Robbie was tough as nails, and just as direct as Jimmy with his communication, which explained why they were best friends. Robbie had been with the show over ten years, and he knew exactly how it needed to be shot, as well as how to keep a level head. Robbie would have me practice jumping out of the rental car during the day, as well as running around the parking lot, and then we would go in and break down the shots on how I could improve them.

To give you some perspective on this insanity, I need to offer some inside information on exactly what made this difficult. First off, the camera we would be shooting on was a huge camera. It was similar to what you would see watching a TV news show, when you see the camera guy holding something on his shoulder that was about three times the size of his head! The camera sits on your shoulder, and you look into a viewfinder similar to a periscope on a submarine. Your left hand then holds the camera from a strap that is attached to the front lens, and has toggle levers so you can control zoom in and out points, as well as focus. This allows you to push in on whatever you are shooting, and then pull back out to a wide shot to show the entire environment. You can do this by simply moving forward or back with your left hand finger on the lens toggle lever.

My first thought was why are we using these massive cameras, but once I understood that the smaller cameras do not allow the easy use of zoom control, it made sense. Langley started the show using these cameras, and really no reason to stop using the same camera. It's kind of one of those "if it's not broke don't fix it" scenarios.

The good news for me at this time, was the usual squad car was a Ford Crown Victoria that had a large cabin space, and I, as a large man, still fit quite well. Even with the camera, I can fit in the passenger seat, and am able to roll left to right going from the driver to the front windshield. This allowed me to get the introduction of the call, and then pan to the front of the car and zoom in to see the action. This was part of the standard COPS intro.

The other part of this practice would be to include not just the panning left to right of the camera in car positioning, but the fact that when the shit hits the fan, you have to be able to jump out of the car like Lightening McQueen or Flash Gordon (if your old enough to understand that). The trick with this was to situate yourself in the passenger seat, and be able to hold the camera in your right hand and use your left hand, as well as your right foot, to make this exit work. The normal procedure would be placing your right foot against the bottom door panel, and using your left hand to reach across your body

49

when the situation was needed to open the door handle. As soon as you released the door handle, you would use your foot to push open the door so you could jump out and reposition yourself standing to continue shooting. This in itself took some time to practice around the hotel parking lot, and imagine the poor bastard who was just parking and checking in for an insurance seminar to witness this crazy crap! Some insane man running through the hotel parking lot with a camera? Yeah, next! I would have totally got another hotel.

Robbie really helped me get more comfortable shooting the show, and we also became great friends. Robbie would defend me to Jimmy and post as we worked together, because he would tell them, "When I give him something to work on each night, he would and it would improve. He listens to me and takes good direction." This helped me to keep working and really learning the show, and how to properly shoot it. Robbie and I wound up working several venues together over the next couple of years, because we worked so well together, and also had fun.

After the first season ended, I had really started to understand the system. Running as fast as you can with a 40-pound camera while trying to maintain composition, focus, and most importantly, keeping your ass from falling to the ground is no easy task. But once you, as the cameraman, understood the show and how it was shot, it all kind of falls into place.

So……

Today is YOUR day to work on COPS! I want to put you in the driver's seat and explain how we shoot the show so you have a real perspective and understanding of a day in the life of a COPS cameraman. Most people who have watched COPS over the last twenty years or so, have probably wondered how this show works, and how they managed to get over twenty years of broadcasts out of it. So here we go…

The day starts with the normal roll call at the precinct. My sound guy and myself will sit in a room with all of the deputies for the evening shift, before we go out on the road. This is when we discuss any specific events that might be going on that evening. Maybe a concert, or an event that might have a traffic diversion. We also discuss any "bolo's" (be on the lookout) that might be prevalent, and anything else that might need to be addressed that evening before the shift starts. After all the updates have been discussed, the team will then leave the building and get into their squad cars, and start the evening shift. We would get in the car with our officer or sheriff, and sometimes this is a normal marked car, or other times it is an unmarked car. It really just depends on the officer we are riding with, and what vehicle has been issued to them. I would sit in the passenger seat of the car, and my sound guy would sit in the backseat. Once we leave the department and start our evening shift, usually we will stop off to fill up the gas tank. Sometimes this is a specified county fuel station, or other times it's actually at the local convenience store. Usually, the deputy or officer will have a county credit card for fuel. If we fill up at the latter, we will grab a Red Bull or soft drink to start the evening off. Now we are off to the races! The first part of the shift usually starts pretty slow, and we can all get comfortable and ready to get a story or two. If we have ridden with this officer before, and have a rapport with them, then it's just some catching up. But if this is our first night riding with this individual, then I will explain exactly how we shoot the show, what calls make great stories, and how we always want to represent the department in a professional manor. It takes a couple of nights to really get a new officer to be comfortable with us for obvious reasons. Hell, I would not want a camera stuck in my face all night while just trying to do my job! I found that the best way for me to get a new officer to get comfortable with us riding with them, was to tell them right at the beginning, "My job is to shoot a great story for you to be able to show your family and friends for years to come." If they had a family, I would tell them that it would be great for their children to be able to watch Daddy getting the bad guy! This usually allowed them to realize that as a film crew, we really did want to show them in a great light, and just want to have a safe and enjoyable evening. Once we get the early evening dialogue finished, we would start our night. As we ride, we listen to dispatch for any calls, while our officer follows cars and runs plates to see if they have an expired tag or a broken taillight. We look for any reason to legally pull over a vehicle, because you never know what you will find during the stop. Dispatch is fully aware that the film crew is riding with this officer, and will send all high priority calls to them first so we can try to get a story. While we wait to get that dispatch, we just look for anything that looks suspicious, like drug deals on the street corner, or broken business windows, or as a last resort, the expired tag or broken tail lights. When we pull a car over or have a dispatch call, my job is to start shooting, and the first thing we would shoot would be an explanation of the call. So to start the video, I would lean to the left with my camera on my shoulder, and have my camera on the police officer, as he or she would tell us what we were about to be doing. This may be pulling over a vehicle for an expired tag, or it may be pulling up to a home for a domestic disturbance call. Regardless, the introduction would usually always be the same. "We are going to pull this car over for an expired tag and see why they are still driving it." Or, "We just received a call from dispatch that a domestic violence situation is occurring, and we are right around the corner." When you watch the show, this is usually how a story starts out, and of course the words are printed in the lower left corner saying "Domestic Disturbance 9:30 pm." Regardless, the template was the same, and that was what we were hired to do. It was easy for me to get out of the front seat of the car, but my soundman had to have a leash. With this simple dog leash, he would be able to roll down the window an inch, and thread the leash down to the handle. Using a clip that attached to the outside door handle, he would pull on the leash from the inside of the car, and it would lift up the outside door handle so he could exit. Did I mention that police car rear doors will not open from the inside? I'm pretty sure this is a no brainer, but I never knew that before I started the show.

As the stop or call progresses, I would try to cover the action from as many angles as I could without panning all over the place. I learned from Jimmy that the best thing to do to cover dialogue is since the cop is usually standing next to the person they are talking to, then start on a two-shot and slowly zoom into each one. Get the good talking points, and then zoom back out to the two shot, then push in for reactions and such. If the talking goes on for a while, then periodically pan over the police car door emblem, or anything the editors can use as a transition. A transition is just anything the editors can use to shorten the scene. This entire segment cannot be any longer than seven minutes front to back, so a shot of the car door can be used quite well. Let's say the two are talking, and the person being questioned starts rambling on for ten minutes about why he or she does not have a current driver's license. The editors can start the scene, and before the person in question starts rambling on, it cuts to the car door so the editor can cut out all of the rambling. Then they get back to the arrest, or foot pursuit, or sometimes just letting them go, but unless there is a good reason this would not normally make a show. I would shoot every event like it would become a broadcast aired show, no matter how boring or uneventful the stop seemed to me, because you never know when something is going to happen. If you do not have all of your shooting elements in place, the editors will not be able to put a show together.

After the show is complete, and they are handcuffed and sitting in the back of a car (not our car, we would have another officer show up to transport), then I would set down my gear and work on getting the releases. Usually this required me getting in the back seat with the individual, so they could not say at a later time that they were pressured because they were next to the cop. They call this "under the color of authority", and it happened many times to many shooters over the years, so you learn it's just better to have the conversation cameraman to arrested man, or woman. Safety was also a critical element that needed to constantly be monitored while maintaining composure. Since this show was real, and nothing was staged or rehearsed, you always had to keep an eye on your surroundings as well as your camerawork. I really started to understand why Jimmy pushed my demo reel aside that one day last year. This really was not like any other job I had ever done, and any cameraman who would be hired for this show would sort of be starting at the beginning.

The biggest key to being a good shooter is enjoying what you are shooting, and I really enjoyed shooting this show.

During my time with COPS, I witnessed things most people will never see. I have been in the passenger seat of a cop car going 120 mph chasing bad guys, that turned into full out foot pursuits. I have been on K9 tracks in the ghettos, chasing drug dealers. I have been on scene after murders, suicides, floaters in the river, and gang shootings. Alternatively, I have also wanted to laugh so hard while shooting because something was so funny, but I had to stop myself so my laughter would not make TV. Some shows that made air were really good shows, some were less great, but I'm glad they made broadcast. Working with Robbie, I not only was getting some great camera footage, but I also definitely got better at getting people to sign releases! Most importantly, I was becoming really confident in my shooting ability, and was grateful for this experience!

One particular show I remember shooting with Robbie, was a 17-year-old female (a minor) who had assaulted her boyfriend. It wasn't major, but the assault

54

had caused some scratches on his arm and chest, and the cops were called. When we showed up, she was kind of smart-mouthed and funny, and it did make an interesting story so I kept shooting, but eventually both the parents showed up. They, of course, were less than pleased to see the COPS crew shooting this, and told us to get off the property immediately, which we did. Robbie, the deputy and I all gathered together to discuss how we were going to possibly get this release. The problem was that both Mom and Dad worked in influential positions within the city, and the last thing they wanted was to see their child on TV being arrested. Perfectly understandable, and we knew this would be a tough one.

An average show only lasts roughly seven minutes, that's how they fit three shows in one twenty-two minute episode. So, no matter how long it takes us to shoot content for a show, sometimes two hours, they have to condense it down to seven minutes. I took this knowledge and spoke with the parents. The mom had no interest in speaking with me, but I was able to talk to the dad. While we were talking, I mentioned that she had a bit of an attitude and he smiled, laughed, and agreed that was how 17-year-old girls are. So my retort was simple and clear, I told him, "Listen, sir, you have been trying to teach your daughter humility for the last 17 years, I can teach it to her in seven minutes! When all of her friends see her on TV being snotty, it's not going to look good, and she will have to own that for years to come." He smiled again and said, "Let me talk to my wife." Five minutes later, I had signed releases from them, as well as the minority release, and that show still airs.

Another show that was a lot less than fun was when we were called out to a possible suicide. It was in a trailer park, and as we pulled up, we could see the obvious, a man in his late 30's had put a revolver to his head on the front porch of his girlfriend's home. The man had also lived in the community, and had decided to end his life that night. He was lying on his back, with blood flowing out of his head, and the pistol was lying by his side. This was obviously not going to be a show because he was dead, or at least dying, and there was no crime. It was clearly self-motivated, and tragedy is not what makes entertainment. This would just be one of those calls that all I could do would be to help anyway I could. I put the camera down and assisted as best I could. A girl came up and told us she was his lover, but she had another boyfriend, and that the man on her porch had called her earlier in the day and told her he was going to kill himself.

He had earlier in the day left a note on her doorstep, which she said she never read, and had just thrown it in the dumpster at the end of the street. The man's dog was running through the property in a crazy way, clearly upset and lost because his daddy was not moving. As the police processed the scene, I offered to go over to the dumpster and see if I could find the suicide letter. I walked down the street, climbed into the dumpster with my flashlight, and rummaged through the garbage. I did eventually find the letter wrapped up in a bag of vegetables and fruits. While I was lifting it out with my extendable baton, so as to not impair the evidence, I heard the worst sound ever. Because only a few deputies were on scene, no one was able to get a hold of the dog, and it had run out into the street in hysteria and was hit by an oncoming car. All of us looked at each other and knew what had just happened, and it was so saddening. Neither the man, nor his dog, made it through the night.

This was the hardest part of working on this show, as we are not cops; we are camera people, trying to make a living. We are not trained to handle horrible situations on a daily basis, and yet at the end of each shift, we go back to our hotel rooms and try to become normal again. Day after day, event after event: suicide, hanging, gang shooting, motorcycle accident, industrial accident, homicide, or a welfare check when someone just dies at home alone after having a brain aneurism because of a medical condition. The cops are somewhat trained to expect and handle these situations, but the crew are not. Either we find our off switch every night back at the hotel, or we don't, and that's why so many crewmembers quit the show. It gives me such great respect for the officers, because finding the off switch cannot be easy, whether you are trained or not.

Most of the time I was able to find my off switch, and the longer I shot the show, the more able to cope with it I became. But I can tell you, I still dream about some of those awful experiences, and I still wake up really sad sometimes. The hardest to deal with by far was when it was a child related case. You never get over that!

Part of being a field producer/cameraman is not only knowing how to perform your skills, but also knowing how to be empathetic and letting that human emotion be a part of your job. With COPS, it was critical. I realized early on that, once again, humility is so much more effective than ego. When I first started with COPS, I developed an ego almost from day one. I was a cameraman for COPS, the number one show on primetime TV. I was on top of the world. I must be awesome!

Well…no, and I learned that pretty quickly, especially when it came time to get releases. Just my body language at the beginning was clearly obvious, and no one would sign a release. Why would they? Some cocky large dude with a camera is now trying to get a release after they just had the worst day of their life! Who would sign that? I wouldn't!

Another shooter I met while on the show was Chris Flores, and he sat me down one night, and with his words of wisdom, opened up my eyes to the world of COPS. He told me, "Listen, when I first started the show I felt awesome too. I had my vest, and had a belt with a flashlight and stuff. I looked like a cop so I felt like a cop, and it was awesome! The sooner you can remove that emotion from your gut and become just a simple cameraman doing a job to support your family, the sooner people will see the real empathetic side of you and sign releases! Just remove the attitude, you're NOT a cop and empathize with their situation, then they will sign."

Chris was so right. Once I chilled out and started talking to these individuals like human beings, as opposed to talking at them like they were criminals and I was Superman, they would start talking to me. They wouldn't always sign, but more often than not, they actually would. Just to be absolutely clear, the hardest part of getting the release was we couldn't offer them money, a lesser charge, or even not to tow their car. We had absolutely zero control on the traffic stop, or domestic charge, or drug possession, or any infraction whatsoever. We had no offering capability at all. We just had to have the ability to talk with them, and ask them to sign. That's all, and if we couldn't get the signatures, we couldn't get the shows, and then we would not be working for much longer. So, as COPS shooters, we were always kind to all parties, and that helped me immensely during my tenure with the show. The releases started coming in, and my shows started to air. I have been involved in so many situations while working on COPS, and have developed some of the most amazing friendships with law enforcement along the way. I stay in contact with deputies and officers all around the country still, and I would not have had the opportunity to develop these friendships had I not worked on this show.

Some of my more memorable venues while working on COPS were Tulsa, Oklahoma; Tampa, Florida; and West Palm Beach or Belle Glade, for sure. Not just because of the constant calls and craziness of the night, but because of the friendships I made along the way.

Here are some of the memories I have documented from some of my favorite locations during my tenure with COPS.

Tulsa, OK

In June of 2009, they sent us to Tulsa, Oklahoma for a two-month venue. I did not have Robbie as my sound guy this time; I had a gentleman named Carlos who was just starting out. Robbie was working with another cameraman one town over, so we all stayed in the same hotel, and could review footage at night. Robbie and I knew that on our days off we could still do things together, like play basketball or race go-karts. We would usually look up a local go-kart race track in town, as we really enjoyed racing.

When we first pulled up to the Tulsa County Sheriff's office, we were greeted with open arms by the department! This was the first time COPS had shot in Tulsa, and they were very excited to see what we could do for Tulsa recruitment. Tulsa County sheriffs compete closely with the local police department, and this was kind of a friendly competition as to which division would get the most stories. Robbie was with the Police Department, and I was with the Sheriff's Office.

The chief's name was George Harrelson, and he was happy to welcome us into his department and offer us anything we needed to help show the Tulsa Sheriff's Office in its best light. It's really nice when you have such a cooperative venue, as it does lift everyone's moral, and helps us get great stories. When we first met in the chief's office, he presented us all with Chevron patches, these are the side patches that say Tulsa sheriff's office. Then we all went down to administration, and had photo IDs made, representing us as working with Tulsa. Not all departments do this, so it is always nice when you have an ID for memorabilia.

The next day when we all met in his office, he had replica sheriff's cars in display cases for all of the crew. We all knew this was going to be a really fun venue to work. George was very proactive, and would show up on most calls to make sure all protocol was proper, as you never want to misrepresent the department on national TV. Tulsa is an amazing place, and for the COPS crew, it was even better, because the county is so vast and most homes are built acres apart and miles from town. So when you had a priority call, you would frequently have a ten to fifteen-minute code run, meaning lights and sirens flashing, and racing at speeds above 100 mph. This is always an adrenaline rush for us. We did shoot quite a few stories during our Tulsa venue.

I remember riding around with our deputy on the outskirts of Tulsa one day, and stopping by a community boat ramp area just to say hello to one of the other deputies working off duty. Tulsa is a beautiful place, with large open fields, and large lakes for boating and fishing. We had pulled into the parking lot and were chatting with the off-duty deputy. Out of the blue, a white pickup truck rolled past us slowly. The off duty deputy recognized the driver, who was clearly intoxicated by not only the massive amounts of crushed cans in the bed of the truck, but by the way he was almost scraping our car. He damn near pinned the cop between us and the truck! As he was pulling forward, and the other deputy started to tell him to pull to the side and get out of the truck, he gunned the gas, and headed out of the park!

The next thing you know, we are chasing a drunk driver down country roads, while my deputy was calling in the pursuit to dispatch, so we could eventually get some backup for this hopefully inevitable stop. One small issue with this show, was I was not shooting when the situation first started, as he came up from behind and the camera was in my lap. So as soon as the craziness started, I threw the camera on my shoulder and our deputy started the reason for the call. This happens every now and then, because you just never know when the shit is going to hit the fan. We chased the truck for several miles and our cop knew the road was about to come to an end up ahead, so he told us to "pucker up" and get ready to run. The truck finally pulled off the road before the road closed sign, and the driver opened the door and started running into an open field. He was able to jump over the cow pasture fence even though he was plastered, so we did the same. One of my thoughts at the moment was how impressed I was with this guy's dexterity for being drunk as a skunk, and the other was "is that cow shit I just stepped in?" The pursuit ended with a taser deployed, and our bad guy on the ground. I have never personally been tased, some of the crews have just to experience the sensation, but I'm just not that daring and was willing to take their word for it that it sucked! By this time, we had backup, so each deputy took an arm or leg to carry him out to the car. When we loaded him in the car, and they asked him why he did this, his response was, "I'm already dead." This became the title of the story we submitted to Langley. The chief was happy, as we had another good story, and the deputies were all happy with the arrest, while I scraped cow shit off my boots. In a situation like this, we have to wait five hours after the arrested individual is processed and out of the hospital, since during the arrest they were intoxicated, they are not in the proper frame of mind to sign a release. We drove to the jail later that evening, and I was able to get a signed release.

Tulsa, of course, also provided fun stories about lost cows in the road. Which apparently prompted for radio communication with the dispatcher to say funny things over the air on camera, like the suspect is "Moooving" south on S.R. 64. Too much fun! Unfortunately, as with most venues, Tulsa also had some very tragic calls. One in particular, I will never forget, would be an autistic child who was missing from home.

His family had called in because he had just slipped away and they could not find him. As I said, most properties on the outskirts of Tulsa are very large, consisting of many acres and neighbor's properties are the same.

When this family called, we were dispatched to the location and immediately started a perimeter search around the property. Because of the severity of this situation, most cars were called in, unlike what would usually happen, as we are normally first on scene to get a show. I did not shoot this, as it would never be a story. First, because he was a minor, but more importantly, he was autistic and that would never air out of respect for the child and the family. So, my sound guy and I just assisted the best we could to help find this child.

We searched all around the property with the homeowners and did not find the child, so as other deputies were continuing the yard search, we chose to expand to the neighbor's house down the street. The neighbors had a pool in their backyard, and as we walked around the front of their house, we were able to see the backyard pool and, tragically, the body of a young boy lying at the bottom of the pool.

The deputy I was with immediately dropped his belt, and jumped in to try and rescue the little boy. I waited at the edge of the pool to help lift the child out. He was not breathing, and as we pulled him from the water and laid him on the ground, my deputy started CPR as the other deputies started running across the street to administer aid as well.

I held the child's hand and tried to talk to him while CPR was being administered, and the paramedics were en route.

The four-year-old child did not make it. He was dead before we even found him at the bottom of the pool. My son was almost three years old at the time, and all I could think about was losing my son. The feeling was profound to me, and as a cameraman, I had to take this experience back to the hotel and find a way to turn off that switch. No production company on the planet could really prepare you for this type of fieldwork, and I understand why Langley would go through crew from time to time. This show can be intense and soul crushing at times, and I can honestly say the only way I was able to deal with this that night was a substantial amount of alcohol. Truthfully, this image has stayed with me to this day.

On a brighter note, I think my Uncle Bart's favorite story was also in Tulsa, when we were looking for a domestic suspect who had beaten up his wife and left the home. As we were searching around the mobile home complex, we noticed a large bush that had two cowboy boots sticking out of the bottom. Really? He was just hiding out inside a big bush but kept his boots out thinking they would just blend in? Visualize if you will, a large green bush with snakeskin boots. Yes, this also made a story. After our venue was over with Tulsa, we had a viewing party with all of the deputies we had been riding with, and I have stayed in touch with George through all of these years. He left Tulsa, and is currently working narcotics theft and applying for the U.S. Marshals Office.

George also had one of my personal AR-15 rifles laser engraved with the Tulsa badge on it. What a treat!

Tactical Training

One of the great benefits of working with law enforcement, and developing relationships with the people you are with every day, was my ability to work with the deputies on my days off at the training field. While the other camera crewmembers would play golf on their days off, I would spend time at the range when they would let me, and practice the aspects of tactical response and fortifying procedures. Being a tactical enthusiast, this opportunity was so cool to me. It also helped me secure a lot of trust in the deputies I was riding with, because I was kind of part of the team. I would practice with the staff in the hallways of the department, utilizing crowd control body shields, pushing through the pseudo crowds, and securing forward perimeters. When we were at the range, we would practice walking forward rifle shots, then switching to our sidearm and continuing our shots until the timer sounded. Other times, depending on the budget of the department, we would have custom built barriers on the field to shoot around for cover. I was able to practice with many of the SWAT teams, and to me this was like being a kid in a candy store! One department in particular had the armourer meet us at the range, and I was able to shoot some of the coolest fully automatic weapons money can buy, like the Glock 18 full auto pistol!

Real life education is learned, however, in real life situations. One in particular that comes to mind was in Seattle, Washington. We had received a call from dispatch of a possible potential suicide in progress, meaning an individual had called 911 saying they were going to end their life. This person had a history of doing this in the past, but the more concerning factor was this caller was a retired police officer, who they knew had many guns in his home and the knowledge of how to use them. He was extremely intoxicated based on dispatch's interpretation of the call. Anytime a law enforcement officer, retired or not, is part of the call, special procedures have to be taken. This includes bringing in the SWAT team for added protection.

Before we pulled up to his home, we all grouped up about a block away to discuss what tactical response would be implemented. We had four SWAT members who would lead the call, and then the two deputies we were riding with, as well as myself and my soundman to document the procedure. The decision was made to breach the front entrance alone, as the call stated it was just the one individual, and not a group of people to be concerned with. I felt pretty confident about my training and abilities by this point. However, today I had a camera on my shoulder, not a gun in my hand. As we drove up to the property and left our vehicles, my camera was rolling. As always, the team led the call, and myself and my sound guy were in the rear filming, yet staying out of anyone's way. It's one thing to film a great story, but it would be horrible to ever think anyone would get hurt or worse, because the camera crew got in the way of a tactical situation. We were always very cautious of the deputies, and what they were about to do. Everyone should go home safe to his or her family, including the person they are trying to help. As the team entered the house, the first thing we noticed was the two German Shepherds that immediately came running up to us! They were just doing their jobs as protectors of the home, and were scared, of course. They were barking and growling, but one of our SWAT members was also K9, and he was able to get them settled and out of the house, so we could continue finding the caller and administer the help he needed.

The mindset of law enforcement can be difficult, because their job is to protect and serve, yet sometimes they also have to make quick decisions to save their own life, which may mean ending someone else's.

As we cleared the top floor of the house, and did not find the caller, we started down the stairs to the lower first floor. The house was on a hillside, so the front door actually opened up to the second floor, and the first floor dropped down to the lower part of the hill. The lower floor, however, had all of the lights off. It was starting to get dark outside, so it was getting really dark inside. The tactical procedure for entering a narrow corridor, like a hallway, is called "two by two cover formation". This means the first cop will open a door, and the cop behind him will enter the room to clear it. Then, the two cops behind them will step upfront and do the same thing. So, as a team, they basically hopscotch down the corridor, until all rooms are cleared. Because of the confusion with the dogs, I wound up in between the team with my camera. So when we got to the bottom hallway, I backed into the first door available to the left, so the team could regroup and proceed with their tactical movement. What I did not even think about until that very second, was this entire hallway was almost pitch black, and the room I had just backed into had not yet been cleared! I was trying to allow my deputies to regroup, because I had got in the way, but I was now in a very unsafe and un-cleared room in the home of a person who was labeled a signal 20 (possible crazy person). The room I had backed into was pitch black, and as I was looking forward into the hallway, it was at that moment it hit me. Holy shit! With all of my practical training, and all of the books I have read, and how prepared I thought I was as a team member, I was really just a cameraman who just backed into a room without thinking. What was going to be next? A cold steel blade across my throat from behind? A straight plunge into my back? A muzzle placed to the back of my head, with that final shot ending my world in a nanosecond?

The situation would go on, and who knows how it would end, but for me the ending would be there and now, and that's it. So many thoughts went through my mind in those very brief seconds, as I realized the major tactical faux pas I had just made. So I spun around, and turned on my camera light to illuminate the room I was so clearly worried about. The room was clear and empty, except for some boxes of stuff. No bad guys with knives and guns, thank God! As the team cleared the hallway, they did find the caller in a room at the end of the hallway, and he had passed out on the couch. No guns, just the TV on, and a bottle of whiskey on the floor sideways, dripping out on the carpet. What is interesting, is how many times we enter a home and COPS is playing on the TV. Not this time, but in general, it did become pretty common.

West Palm Beach / Belle Glade

I have shot in West Palm Beach several times over my tenure with COPS, and we have had some really crazy adventures. One that comes to mind, and this is truly a lesson to every young aspiring cameraman, would be the time we were rolling around looking for bad guys and stories. We were riding with a special tactical team in an undercover Chevy Trailblazer. A call came over the radio that someone had just robbed a 7/11 around the corner by gunpoint, and had left with the money. The team I was riding with said we would definitely see them soon, because we were right around the corner, and this was the closest way to get on I-95. The guys we were riding with were sure that would be where they would be heading. Well, they were right! Before I knew it, a silver, four-door sedan came racing past us to get onto the on-ramp of I-95. I grabbed the camera and started shooting, looking through my eyepiece intensely, as I could see the car in front of us racing, since we were now chasing him with lights and sirens. The chase was on! He was crossing back and forth between lanes, passing cars, and driving crazy. I knew this was going to be a great A story. We were going about 120 mph right next to him, as he intentionally tried to ram us on the passenger side, which was my side!

This was a bit of a hairy moment for me, as I never wear a seatbelt, because I have to be able to get out of the car quickly when they run. So I knew if he actually rammed us and made us flip, I would have no protection, and would most probably be thrown out of the car and killed. Thankfully, my cop was a great defensive driver, and swerved out of the way as to avoid impact from the obvious intention. We slowed down a bit after that, and let him stay in front of us while he was trying to get away, but his engine started to fail. I remember looking through the viewfinder to see black pellets and oil start hitting our windshield. His motor was blowing apart, and small fragments of stuff were starting to come out of his exhaust. These small pieces of motor were now hitting our windshield as his car started to slow down, because the motor was blowing up and could not keep combustion. As the car slowly pulled over to the side of the interstate, it finally stopped. As soon as it did, the bad guy jumped out, and started running down the freeway. We jumped out and chased him, until he was tackled to the ground. I shot the entire event, ending with the suspect in handcuffs and placing him in the car. Then we shot the interviews with the cops, who were so excited, because not only did they get the bad guy, they knew they had an awesome show.

Everyone was stoked about this one. This guy was a felon with multiple warrants, and had just done an armed robbery, so he was most definitely going back to prison.

What a great show! Well…it would have been. One thing that can naturally happen as a camera operator, is when your adrenaline gets high, you can have a tendency to do what we call a "double tap." This basically means that in the heat of the moment you push the record button on the side of the camera, but you also push it again by accident, because you are so pumped. And that's exactly what had happened. Every cameraman will have one of these in their lives. When I pushed the record button twice, I turned the camera record off, but my brain and eye never noticed that the little red light in the viewfinder was not on. So I just kept shooting, because I was so focused on the action taking place in front of me. As I was looking through the viewfinder, I never looked at the information to see if I was recording! I did not notice I had double-tapped until I went to review the footage, and then realized there was a start and an end but no middle. All of the good stuff was missing. Oh crap!

My only saving grace from this major malfunction, was the bad guy would not sign a release. I did ask him, even though I knew I had no show, but his response was so powerful. He said he would not sign a release, because if any of his people saw him on this show, then they would know where he lived, and he would surely be killed. He was such a bad guy, people would kill him in a second if they could find him! How can you argue with that? I want a show, but I don't want it to be the reason someone is killed.

Everyone on the crew wanted to see the footage of the amazing car chase I had shot that night. At the end of the night in the hotel room, of course, I had to explain to them that I double-tapped, but they all understood. Most of them laughed, and said, "Yeah, been there, done that!" More importantly, they really understood when I explained the reason I would have never gotten a release.

Ontario, California

After working on this show for the amount of time I had, my friends would always ask me, "What is the most memorable story you have?" I would reply first with, "pick a category," but then I would usually tell them this one, for sure.

We were shooting in Ontario, California during the summer. Ontario is a very hot and very dry environment in the summer, so it is critical that you can keep cool when possible. It is not uncommon for the heat index to get over a hundred, and with the dry heat, it seems even hotter. We would stay cool in the car by using a neat little gadget called a Cool Cop. This was a plastic hose that would attach to the air vent in the car, and then you could place the other end under your shirt and bulletproof vest to help the cold air keep your chest cool.

When we first started this venue, we met all of the deputies and introduced ourselves, met at lineup, and started riding with them. Each venue we ride at is unique, and that is what makes the job so enjoyable. The people you meet, and the memories you develop along the way. Ontario was just as enjoyable, and one of the fun commonalities of this venue was the Monster energy drink. All of the deputies loved their energy drinks, and the drink of choice for our troops was Monster Green Apple. I had never tried a Monster energy drink, and I will say the Green Apple flavor was awesome!

Every day after lineup we would go to the local food mart to fill up the tank and grab a Monster. After the first or second week of this becoming a daily thing, I went to the store on one of my days off to stock up on food for the week. Our hotel rooms were always extended stay rooms, so they had a small kitchen to make food and coffee before or after a night of shooting. While shopping, I grabbed a six pack of Monsters, why not? They were certainly tasty. One morning after waking up and having my coffee, I opened up a Monster and guzzled it down. Then later in the day before work, I had another after eating some lunch. When we got in the rental car to go to work, my sound guy had one in the cup holder for me. Why ever not? It's a Monster kind of day, I guess! We went to lineup, and then got on the road, filled up the tank, and got another Monster to start our evening of stories and fun. It was particularly hot that day, and we were breaking heat records. We all agreed to not try to pull over anyone unless necessary, as it was just too friggin' hot outside! Stay in the car where it is cool, until needed. As we drove around the city, we were chatting and looking for bad guys, but it was a pretty quiet day. I think it was even too hot for the bad guys to come out!

While we were driving, I started to notice the strangest sensation come over me. As hot as it was outside, and as hard as the car air conditioner was trying to keep up, I started getting chills. Before long, I was actually cold, and was removing the Cool Cop from my chest to try and warm up. The next thing that happened was way more concerning, as I felt an immediate heart palpitation, like someone had just punched me in the chest!

Oh, this sucks! I truly hope that goes away soon. But no, another one. BOOM, then another! I was freezing cold now, and was having a palpitation every five minutes or so. Just long enough between punches for me to think they had ended, then another one again. My sound guy was telling a story about something, I don't remember what. He was just talking, and the deputy we were riding with was listening and laughing, but it was all in slow motion for me, as I was kind of dying in the passenger seat!

There comes a time when as a man, you have to decide whether to either man it up and just stay quiet hoping the pain will go away, or start crying like a little bitch! Yeah, I chose the latter. I told our cop, "Hey, just saying, if I drop over dead, can you please rush me to the emergency room? I'm having some real bad heart palpitations, I think." It was then my sound guy asked how many Monster drinks I had had that day. "I don't know? Four or five?" I replied.

Holy Crap! He said, "Dude! You're only supposed to have no more than two a day! No wonder you are having heart issues!" My cop agreed, with even more kind and supportive words. "Yeah, you're a total dumb shit dude! You need to go lay down and hope you don't have a full-fledged heart attack." As comforting as my two partners were for me, we did agree to just drive around and not try to get into a foot pursuit unless necessary. I was able to settle down after a couple of hours. Thankfully, we did not have to jump out of the car and go into a full sprint run that night, because I truly believe had we done that, I would not be writing this now. LOL! Moral to this story: read the warnings on energy drinks, or do what I do now, and just never drink one again.

Belle Glade, Florida

In my career as a cameraman, I have shot in just about every city in the United States. New York, Chicago, Detroit, But whenever someone asked me, "What is the craziest place you have ever shot?" I have to say Belle Glade, Florida. Belle Glade is located in south central Florida, basically in the middle of nowhere. It is located at the south end of Lake Okeechobee, and between West Palm Beach and Fort Myers, Florida. I will preface this story by stating that most of the people in Belle Glade are great, hard-working people. But as with most low income cities, there are also a significant number of drug dealers and bad people. The main roads across the state are State Road 27 and Interstate 98, and if you did not get off on the side road to go into Belle Glade, you would miss it (Thank God). I'm not writing this book to give happy reviews about locations, so I will just be honest. Belle Glade is a scary place. Google it, if you want. The city is decrepit, and looks so similar to Somalia, we called it "Little Mogadishu". There are buildings with no power, no roofs, and basically poverty-ridden. My issue with Belle Glade is the crime rate is insane! The city is basically populated by either Haitians who are working the cornfields, or drug dealers who are working the streets. Truth is, if you drive down the wrong road into Belle Glade, you could most likely be robbed or car jacked, especially at night.

My first experience with this not-so-quaint town, was driving out of the parking lot of the sheriff's office and driving up to vehicular homicide. A young lady had run over another young lady because "She was messing with my man!" This happened in the middle of the day, and with many witnesses. She just did not care. This is kind of the attitude of the town, they just kill each other. I found this completely insane! We did not get many shows out of Belle Glade, because murders are not shows. We want a bad guy, not a dead guy. Again, please believe me when I say there are so many wonderful people in Belle Glade, hard workers and good people, However, there are a lot of bad people, gangsters and drug dealers that make their drug deals in West Palm and Miami, but are based out of Belle Glade. I can only assume that because of its centralized location, it's like a hiding place for bad guys.

Many professional NFL players have come from Belle Glade or Pahokee, which is a good thing. But the violent calls for service, and the highest number of cases of AIDS per capita for Florida, is not a good thing. I have so many stories from Belle Glade, but truthfully, few made it to TV. Sadly, most of them were fatal and tragic. Honestly, it's just not the kind of place I would want to raise my family. Google "Dem Damn Dogs" if you want validation of the town.

The last day we were filming, we came upon a teenager who was running through the streets with a table leg with nails driven through it, sticking people in the head. WTF?

I was able, however, to really gain some serious tactical experience rushing homes, and learning skills for perimeter points. I also made some amazing friends working Belle Glade, as we always had each other's backs.

Belle Glade also offered many experiences that were memorable, not just because of the crazy calls for service, but also just because of the environment. The fact that the town is so rundown and decrepit, did make you feel bad for the children growing up in this town. That's the sad thing, as the families are mostly single-parent families, with several children and a lot of drugs. Because Belle Glade also has the highest number of cases of AIDS per capita in the United States, we had to be very careful picking up syringes on the street, or dealing with bleeding victims. It's a shame to me how the city of West Palm Beach has let this small part of their community down. I know they are trying, but how do you fix an isolated area of major drug activity, poverty, and crime?

It's kind of like when England boated all of their criminals to Australia. One of our seasoned cameramen threatened to quit if he was scheduled to shoot Belle Glade again. He had worked there twice before, and said he would never work there again. When they scheduled him for the third time with my crew, he revolted and screamed enough, that they put him in West Palm instead. I certainly can't blame him.

A couple of my good friends, James Barka and Charlie Waters, work there. We had worked together so many times, that we became very close friends. James just retired from K9, and is now moving to North Carolina to hunt and fish. Charlie is still working Pahokee, just south of Belle Glade, earning a check and trying to keep the peace. I think Charlie will work there forever, because he enjoys it and has a senior position.

The biggest lesson I learned while shooting several tours in Belle Glade, was being way more aware of my surroundings. Belle Glade was an environment where anything could happen, and I wanted to get back home safely every night. Truthfully, I was a bit scared the first season I worked Belle Glade, but after the third season, I was very aware of the venue I was in. Langley had us all sign an affidavit stating that we, as camera crew, would not carry firearms. But my thought was, I would rather be judged by twelve, than carried by six. I understand why Langley would not want the liability if any of their crew used a firearm during a scheduled shoot, but to be placed in this type of environment and not have any way to protect yourself if needed, to me, became the choice of that crewmember.

James Barka, K9 Six and I went through some crazy times together during my West Palm episodes. He was part of the K9 unit, and his dog at the time was named Chip. Chip was an amazing German Shepherd, and all James wanted was to get his dog on TV before he had to retire him! The last time we worked together was with a new crew, and I was hoping we could finally get Chip on a show. We did! It was awesome. It became a two-camera crew, as my team was in West Palm, and another team was shooting in Belle Glade. A trespassing call came over the radio in Belle Glade. I was able to film James in West Palm with Chip getting into the helicopter, while the other crew was waiting at the location for the helicopter to arrive. Barka and Chip jumped into the helicopter to fly to Belle Glade, and the new camera crew filmed them landing and jumping out with Chip, and doing what we call a track. A track is when a dog gets a smell of the perp, and searches the area trying to track the smell. Chip found the suspect, who was hiding under a building. He was able to clutch onto his leg, and literally drag him out from under the building far enough so the deputies could reach him.

It was a good arrest and a great show. Chip got to be in a show, and James was very happy. It made for a great night. I have always enjoyed working with K9 units whenever the department will allow us, as I believe dogs are amazing animals! To me, a dog is really an angel sent from God to protect you, and be your best friend. A good dog will always have your back, with no fear or hesitation. Few humans have this intestinal fortitude or unconditional love. I have worked with some amazing K9 units in the past, and so many fond memories of these wonderful animals. If a K9 dog is killed in the line of duty, they get the same funeral procession as a human, and it's truly well deserved.

Boynton Beach 7-15-2010

You might remember this one. It's the only "murder for hire" episode I have ever filmed. We had just been sent to Boynton Beach, it was the police department for Boynton this time as opposed to the sheriff's office, as we randomly go between both divisions. The department was awesome as usual, and has had the COPS crew there many times in the past, so they were very used to us being in the cars with them, and were comfortable with how we worked.

The very first day we showed up, one of the lead investigators asked us if we wanted to shoot a murder for hire, which in the legacy of the COPS show we had never done. Of course we were very excited about the opportunity to shoot this show. Jimmy happened to be with us at the time to get us acclimated with the department, so he main-framed the process. They had already wired the "hit man's" car with hidden cameras, as he was an undercover cop, so they were able to record the suspect agreeing to the hit before we ever got to the venue. Weeks of undercover planning and recording had been done to prepare for this day, and how lucky were we to be in the right place at the right time to get this show. I had brought a tripod, which we normally never use, but I had intended to shoot beach shots on my days off and had it in my car. So we decided to act as a "news crew" for the initial set up. The simple deal was this, she had hired a hit man to kill her husband, and the hit was supposed to go down in the early morning, while she was at the local gym working out. Then she would come home to find him dead. Since the PD knew about the situation, because she was actually talking to an undercover police officer and not a hit man, we staged ourselves outside the house to film once she would be coming back home. The police department removed the husband in advance, and staged the scene to look like the hit had happened, and then called her and asked her to come home because "there had been an incident." They placed crime scene tape all around the house, and even parked crime scene vans around the property. All of this had been planned in advance by the police department, but obviously the husband was oblivious to any of this. So when they knocked on his door to explain what was going down, he was totally shocked and confused, of course! We had radio communication with undercover lookouts, so after she received the call from the detective about the problem at home, we were told when she was going to be pulling up and started to roll cameras. Chris took one angle, and I took the longer, tighter angle because I was on a tripod, which made the shot steadier. This allowed me to follow her from a long distance away, and zoom out as she got closer. Once she got out of her car and the detective told her about the situation, I can tell you the hair raised on the back of my neck when she went into acting mode. She just immediately burst into crocodile tears the second the deputy told her that her husband had been murdered, not even a nanosecond to process! The next words out of her mouth was that she wanted to see the body! She wanted proof of the hit! She was such a black widow, and she wanted him dead so she could get his cash.

After she was told about the situation, they took her to the police station to answer questions. Since we had two cameramen on this shoot, Chris and I both were able to shoot many angles and several different things going on at the same time, to get more coverage for the show. This could possibly be the biggest show to hit COPS in years! Chris and I tag teamed to get all of the footage and conversations needed, plus we got the room feeds and in car footage to make the show. The murder for hire footage became one of the very few hour-long COPS shows in history, because of all of the compelling elements. The case was appealed twice, but during the third and final trial she was finally found guilty, and will remain in prison until 2032. Google Dalia Dippolito to read all about it. Talk about just good luck for a production company to show up the day before such a huge bust was going to go down! During the appeals she tried to say that it was all an act, and they were filming a reality TV show, but of course that did not fly with the jury, and her husband denied any of that as well. At least he was alive, because if the person she had met in the car that morning was not an undercover police officer, and a true hit man, her husband would be dead for sure right now.

As we would travel from venue to venue, I would sometimes notice similarities in what I would like to call "the excuse factor". When someone is pulled over, or arrested for whatever reason, the excuses would sometimes get pretty creative. I can understand this, as once you are in handcuffs you will pretty much say just about anything to try and get the police officer to show some form of sympathy, and let you go.

While we were shooting in King County, California. I started to frequently notice a large amount of people we would detain would immediately inform us that they were either a pastor or a minister. Apparently, they thought having this relationship with God would offer them a get out of jail free card? This must have been discussed in the town between the drug dealers, as almost on a nightly basis, we would get at least one individual who would inform us of his divine ordained position. This really became quite comical as we would work our shift, and the process would usually be similar in how the dialogue would go.

Cop- "Good evening sir, the reason I pulled you over tonight is that your license plate is expired. Were you aware of this?"

Person in car- "I'm a minister, thank you." And they would hold up a laminated card stating that they were, in fact, a minister from some church or organization.

Obviously, the officer would maintain his composure, even though myself and my sound guy were laughing quietly to ourselves, as what we all really want to say is that it is not God's responsibility to renew your tag. But for some reason, the people in this town felt it was an easy way out of a ticket. Not only did it not work for them, especially if we found drugs in their pants, but I was surprised to find out just how many ministers would have drugs in their pockets. I'm not saying that these drugs were part of God's plan, but it certainly seemed to be part of the person who held the little laminated card. So one night at dinner, we as a team all decided to become ministers as well, because apparently just about anyone else can! We got online on our cell phones while eating, and found several ministries that will ordain you for $19.95!

To me this was a great deal, as I would not have to go to school, or read a bunch of scripture, or wear a brown robe and shave my head. Just give them my credit card, and get all of the honors and benefits of also having a laminated card. We all signed up, and then after dinner, drove back to the station to print up our brand new certificates! What made this adventure even more fun, was when the next time we would pull someone over and get the usual response, we would all grab our certificates out of our pockets and tell them that we as well were ministers of the faith, and what a crazy coincidence this was? To see their faces was priceless! Certainly worth $19.95!

Another much more frequent excuse that I have heard in just about any venue I would work, was the simple excuse, "See what had happened was…" This would usually be followed with, "Ah, man! These ain't my pants, these are my cousin's pants!" From town to town, this had to be the most common excuse I would hear. Apparently, everyone's cousin was fat, because the pants never fit, and were always hanging down to their knees! My girlfriend will attest to the fact that I am certainly not a fashionista, so I have never really understood the pants hanging way down look, unless everyone who does it just wants to display their expensive Hanes underwear.

A common dialogue between our sheriff and the perp would usually go like this:

Cop- "So can you explain to me where you got the baggie of crack cocaine I just found in your right front pocket?"

Perp- "See what had happened was… these ain't my pants! These are my cousin's pants. No wait! I got these pants at the Goodwill, and they must have had that crack already in the pants! Nobody at the Goodwill told me there was crack in these pants! Damn, that bitch lied to me!"

I have to say, the prolific wording would usually change as the inquisition would continue, but what a real treat to experience from behind the camera lens! If I had a dollar for every time I heard someone say "These ain't my pants", I would be very wealthy right now, for sure. If I was using this phrase in a drinking game, I would be dead! LOL. To this day, my family still uses this phrase whenever we are questioned for just about anything, and it has become the go to at most holiday gatherings.

By the way, I am an ordained minister with the Universal Church of Life, and am allowed all the rights and privileges to perform all duties of the ministry. This is signed my Chaplain B.L. Martin, and for $19.95, I'm sure it's totally legit!

Tampa 2011 Hillsborough County Sheriff's Office

Of all of the venue COPS took me, I would have to say I created the most friendships in Tampa, which makes sense, since I live there. We rode with several deputies, but Chris White and Brian Jackson were the primary deputies we rode with the most. They had an undercover pickup truck with an extended cab, and boy, they knew how to find the bad guys.

Tampa is a melting pot of cultural diversity, and just like most other cities, parts of it are well known for its strip clubs and prostitution, as well as the usual drugs, car thefts, and such. I have lived in Tampa for many years, and I love this town. My studio was in St. Petersburg, which is just across the bridge, and I graduated high school in Tampa. When I first received orders to shoot in Tampa, I was very excited, not just because it was my hometown, but because it also meant I would be home every night. It's nice to be removed from the hotel scene. My sound guy's name was Rhett, whom I had worked with on a couple of venues, so we were already comfortable working together. Rhett was also excited to be working in Tampa, because he was in the process of purchasing a sailboat, and wanted to take a sailing class while he was in town. When we first showed up at roll call, we met most of the deputies we would be riding with. Chris and Brian were on the roster, and when we all met, we knew we would work out great. They were both professional, but funny. They both had a great sense of humor, and knew the streets. Brian was working to get into undercover narcotics, and Chris had been working the streets for years, and just knew the lay of the land.

We started out normal, driving around the "fish bowl" and introducing Rhett and I to the area. The geographical area around central Tampa was located between North Fletcher Avenue and south to Fowler Avenue. Then up past the USF campus, and down to the higher income area of Carrollwood. This looked like a fish bowl if you looked at it from the sky, so it had been coined that way. This is where most of the major crime calls took place, so of course, this is where we spent most of our time waiting for a story.

Every now and then when working on this show, we had the opportunity to work with officers or deputies who had been on the force long enough that they did not have to worry about where to look for bad guys, or how to find them. They just knew exactly where to look, based on years of experience in the streets. Some departments in the past have placed us with rookie cops, because a lot of the seasoned cops would not want a ride along. They were set in their ways, and did not want to get jammed up on camera. This was not the case with Chris and Brian, they had full control of what area to look, in regards to geographical location for finding new stories. They also could create their own work schedule, to offer us the best times to go out and find stories. This allowed the camera crew to also have that freedom to play and find the bad guys.

Specific parts of downtown Tampa, I would learn, are known for transvestite prostitutes. The first week we were riding with Chris, he drove Rhett and I down Fowler and Nebraska Avenue, which is known for these special "ladies of the evening". Quite a bit of illegal activity happens here, so it is a good place to look for a potential story. Brian was off, so it was just the three of us that night. We drove into a parking lot and up to one of the local workers. She was dressed in a mini skirt and tight top, and had a lot of make-up and glitter on. She recognized Chris's car, and had no problem walking up to us. This night we were in a crappy, brown Crown Victoria that looked like it had not run in years, but somehow still moved. She walked up to my window, leaned in, and said hello to us. Chris explained that Rhett and I were both with the COPS TV show and we were shooting locally here in Tampa. She was so excited. "OMG! I LOVE that show! Really? You guys are with COPS?" She reached in and touched my shoulder, as I was in the passenger seat. "I'm Brandy! You're the camera guy for COPS? You're like a rock star!" This did make me feel a little uncomfortable, as I now had a prostitute touching me and admiring my work. I had to giggle a little as I told her, "No, I'm just a cameraman doing my job."

Chris told her we would be working the area the entire month, so if she had anything good to shoot to let him know. "Okay, baby," she said, "I got your number."

I shook her hand and said, "It was nice to meet you, Brandy," and we drove off. Brandy was a fit young lady who clearly was comfortable with the streets. I knew this would be just the beginning of our introductions to the "talent" in the area, an area that I had lived in for ten years, but never knew any of these elements.

I have learned over my time working on this show that the reason a prostitute like Brandy will walk right up to an undercover cop car, is because they really do not feel they are in trouble. And nine times out of ten, they are not. Most of the time, they actually help each other, in the fact that they might have seen someone in the area dealing drugs, or hiding a gun, or things that are much more important to the cop than turning tricks for a living. I'm not saying that it is not illegal to have sex for money, because it is (even though it's the oldest profession in the world), but it's kind of a cat and mouse game. Chris tries to keep the workers safe and off the streets, and the workers try to help Chris catch real bad guys. He does not bully them, or treat them with any ill respect at all, and so they are almost happy to see him pull up to talk.

As we were driving away, Chris pulled into another parking lot and put the car in park so he could power up the computer in the center console. As he was typing up some info, he said, "She's kind of hot, isn't she?" with his normal smirk, like he was about ready to tell a joke. A frequent look from Chris's face, I would soon learn.

I looked at him with a confused expression, as it was obvious she was a prostitute, but I was like, "Yeah I guess?" I was still feeling awkward that she had been touching my shoulder, and had been all affectionate towards me. "Well, check this out Romeo!" he said. I looked at the computer screen in front of me, and it was an array of photos going back to Brandy's first arrest. The strange thing was, back then she was a HE! Brandy was Brandon back in 1998, with a traffic violation at the age of eighteen, and he was a thug-looking gangster. As the arrest pictures continued, you could see an obvious transformation from thug gangster to somewhat pretty lady. Brandon was quite ugly looking as a man, with lip gloss and fake eyelashes, but as the arrest photos continued, it was interesting to see how he became more competent at looking like a she. Because of her career choice, there were so many photos to show the transition, since every time she was arrested, a new photo would be entered into the database.

By the last arrest photo, which was only a month or so prior, she was a full-blown woman, and it would be difficult to tell she was ever a man unless you really looked closely. Chris explained that certain areas of Tampa were huge for this.

I did not notice she was a he when we spoke, and yet she seemed so real and comfortable with what she was doing.

Chris also explained that they would frequently get calls after a John would pull over for sex, and find out that the girl they had hired was actually a guy, and then violently beat them, sometimes to death.

This is a sad situation, considering that one person is working, trying to make money any way they can based on their financial issues, yet the other person who is trying to get a quick blow on the way home, and thinking they are getting something they are not. Both sides are uncomfortable to think about, but that is real life. Sadly, at times that meant the prostitute wound up unconscious in a back-alley, bleeding profusely.

Rhett and I would show up at line up every night, and if we were not with Chris and Brian, we would be with other deputies to roll out and find stories. Tampa deputies, like most other agencies, know the best places to go within their city to find many opportunities to get stories, and we did. One of the first was when we were riding with another deputy named Mark, and we got a call from a bystander about some kids in the park smoking marijuana. We rolled up to the park, and as we were getting out, all of the kids started running away. We chased them, and Mark, who was an amazing runner, caught up with one of the kids who started vomiting once he was caught. Of course, I shot the entire scene and it was an okay film, not great. But it had someone running, getting captured, and puking, and I thought this might make a C category show. So, after Mark cuffed him and put him in the car, then I crawled in and talked to him. His name was Montel, and he was a young kid who was pissed at Mark and I, and not very friendly. Honestly, why would he be? A lot of "Fuck you" went around the car while I was talking to him. I explained that I was with COPS, and although I don't think this will make it to be a show, I have to ask if he would sign a release.

I told him I was just doing my job, and would he sign? This is the hardest part of our job. How do we get people to sign releases when they are already in a heightened state of mind, and now having a really bad day. Of course, they do not want to sign.

As I have said before, we have to be kind, and understand the issue they are going through. If approached with empathy and understanding, I could usually get the release. He finally did sign, and I left the car feeling good, as I usually did when I got a release, knowing that the studio would be happy to consider this a show.

Well, not this time. By the time I woke up the next morning, the local news was all over this story. Apparently, the mom had contacted the news, and was furious because Montel had just turned eighteen, and was only enjoying his new freedom. Why would the police chase him through a park, causing him to puke, and then put him on TV? It became a huge local news deal, and some of the networks were not as law enforcement friendly as other networks. I learned that one anchor had several issues with local law enforcement over the years, so he was not friendly with police in general, and certainly was not going to support our side of the story. This entire situation was new to me, as for some reason I had thought all news channels would support us, as news journalists ourselves. Not so much! The fake news was all about "COPS in town and local unsubstantiated busts!" Our argument was "Why would he run?" He was of legal age, and he was smoking pot in a public park after it was closed. Of course, the studio had to get involved, and state that this bust was not TV worthy, and would not make the show. However, we had every right to shoot and record what we did. Regardless, we had news trucks waiting outside the sheriff's office every day, trying to get shots of the sleazy COPS crew. So we had to get stealthy just trying to leave every day. It was very uncomfortable starting a new venue with all of this drama right out of the gate, as you can imagine. I'm sure the deputies were just as uncomfortable riding with us after that craziness.

Fortunately, we had Brian and Chris, who didn't give two shits. Thank God! We took different cars every day, and sneaked past the TV crews so we could go to work. All of this did blow over eventually, because the show did not air. The kid who ran was of legal age to be arrested, and he did run after getting caught smoking pot in the park after it was closed, and there was really nothing to talk about. The fake news finally just gave up, because they were not going to be able to fabricate a story out of thin air. I learned afterwards that this happens quite a bit all over the States when COPS is in town. It is actually more common than you would imagine. If COPS is in town, and they bust someone on TV, then the family will contact the local news screaming "it was a setup!" Langley has attorneys on retainer just for this.

Bryce Dion, R.I.P.

When I first started out with COPS in 2009, shortly after shooting my first venue, I was sent a plane ticket to meet up with the entire film crew and Langley Productions for a crew/production seminar in Las Vegas. I was still nervous and excited to be working with such a major production company, and absorbing all of the cool new things that went along with such a relationship. I flew in, and rented a car to get to my hotel. I can't remember what hotel it was in Vegas, but it was really nice. I checked in, and got to my room, then went down to the hotel bar to meet up with all of the crew and producers.

Jimmy was there, and it was the first time we were able to chat on a friend level, as opposed to a work level. We had some drinks, and talked about guns as usual. Several other crewmembers were there, also chatting with us. Some of them had been working with the company shooting the show for a decade, and others were brand new.

Bryce Dion was one of the newest, and he was a warm and kind young man. All smiles and laughter, I remember liking him right off the bat. We were both excited about working for COPS, and what it might mean for our future. After a great night, meeting all of the new faces and catching up, we all met in a large convention room the next morning. Bryce sat across from me at the convention table, and we all were engaged with the conversation, led by the panel of seasoned employees including Jimmy, Morgan, and John Langley himself. They discussed shooting techniques, editing transitions, and color balance. They showed us pre recorded episodes on the projection screen of what to shoot, and what not to shoot. They gave us all a nice travel bag full of shirts, DVDs of COPS shows for training, and cool COPS swag. Afterwards, we all met for an amazing dinner at a local restaurant, all paid for by Langley Productions. We all had a great conversation, as we were excited about the upcoming season, and the amazing shows we would create for Langley.

I worked with Bryce a couple of times over my seasons with COPS, but not directly. We would be at the same venue, but on different teams. Bryce was a sound guy, and I was a camera guy, but we were never teamed up together. However, the teams would all meet up for dinner, sometimes with the cops they had worked with. If we had two teams in Tulsa, for example, we would try to schedule our shifts and locations so the two teams could catch up at dinner.

Bryce was very healthy, and I would comment on his healthy eating habits compared to mine. He was consistent about eating salad and healthy foods to stay in shape. He was way more in tune about his diet and food consumption than some of us, but never looked down on any of us for having that third slice of pizza halfway through the night, and I always appreciated that.

Bryce died on August 26, 2014. He was working a venue in Omaha, Nebraska. My understanding from what I have read, was after a routine roll call, he and Michael Lee, the cameraman, headed out for another evening of looking for bad guys. Bryce and Michael were riding with two officers, so they both would have to ride in the back seat. This was not uncommon. Sometimes we would ride with one officer, so the cameraman would ride upfront, other times we would ride with two officers, so we would have to shoot from the backseat. During this evening, they received a call from dispatch saying there was an armed man robbing a Wendy's burger establishment, and it was right down the street from where they were driving.

The call from the dispatch came over the radio so quickly, and they were right around the corner, so they did not have enough time to record an intro. As they were getting out of the car there were people outside saying, "He's inside! Hurry!" Another deputy was outside in the parking lot waiting for backup, and as one officer was going around the back of the building, the other officer and the backup deputy started to go in the front door.

Michael and Bryce were close behind, following the two cops in the front. The front of the building has two doors on either side, going into a small covered room with a front entrance going into the restaurant. In law enforcement, this is called a sally port. It allows the entrance door to close, and then you go into a main front door. For restaurants and burger joints, it's really designed to let people in when it is raining outside, to have a covered space to dry off or place their umbrellas, before they go into the establishment.

As the deputies entered the restaurant, Michael was following close behind with his camera, and opened the first front door to enter the sally port entrance. Bryce was, of course, behind him, following him in. The officers were already in the building, and as they were walking with guns in hand toward the front counter, the armed robber came out from the kitchen with his gun aimed directly at the two officers. The officers fired at him as he was firing at them. Michael immediately ran backwards, since he had just cleared the main door, and fell behind some of the seats. He was able to take cover behind a half wall that has benches.

The camera footage showed Michael acted as quick as he could to find cover, but Bryce was still in the front sally port entrance room. He crouched to take cover, as he was trapped in this front entrance when the shots began.

The armed robber was able to run past the two officers while the gunfight ensued, and ran out of the front door while they were still shooting at him. What no one realized in this split-second moment, was that Bryce was crouched in the entryway, and had been shot. The two officers ran out the front door after the armed robber, and killed him, but it was Michael who got back up and ran to the front door to find Bryce lying on the entrance floor. Bryce had been shot. He ran out the front and told the cops to get an ambulance now! Then went back in the building to take care of Bryce.

All crewmembers for Langley were issued bulletproof vests, and it was mandatory that we wear them. Bryce had his vest on, but apparently a bullet bounced from some other part of the entranceway, and went into his side under his arm, where there is not any protection from the vest.

The bullet went through his underarm and into his chest, probably into his heart. My understanding is that Bryce probably died on scene, but I believe he was pronounced dead at the hospital.

When I decided to move on from COPS, it was for many reasons, but the primary reason was because it was so incredibly dangerous. You can only dance in that type of playground so many times before something really bad happens. Since I had a young son, and had already been in so many close altercations where I was concerned for my personal wellbeing, it was time to leave.

Bryce was killed several years after I had moved on, but all of my friends from COPS called me that evening. We talked about how many close calls we had, and how many opportunities occurred where it could have been us instead of Bryce. COPS, now in its 30th season, has only had one fatality during filming. That in itself is an amazing statistic, considering how often these brave crews go into harm's way, almost on a daily basis, with cracked out hoodlums and crazy psychopaths. Safety is always the primary concern, and the people working on COPS are already very level headed under extreme pressure. It would be normal to say Bryce was just in the wrong place at the wrong time. But the truth is, Bryce was in that bad situation we all had feared, and the outcome became a very tragic ending. Bryce Dion, 38 years old. May he rest in peace. God bless you, my friend.

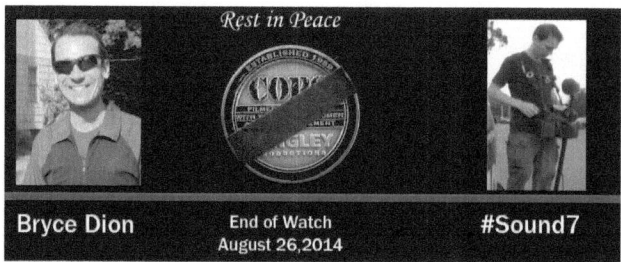

The Punisher

After my second season with COPS, while I was finishing my last week and packing up, I received a phone call from the production company for a new movie called The Punisher. It was to be filmed in Tampa, and they had heard about me from my friend Tommy Hinson. He knew I was a scuba instructor, and the marine unit needed a divemaster to work with them for insurance reasons. I was starting to have some pretty significant back pains, and had seen a doctor about it. I had some MRI's done, and was waiting for the results to come in, but wanted to work on this film. They asked me to contact a man named Rico Browning. Rico leads the industry for marine work in film, and his dad was a film legend. He was one of the original underwater film cinematographers, as well as being many characters in films such as Creature From the Black Lagoon. Rico took over his dad's career, and makes his living as a safety coordinator for feature films. I called Rico, and he told me he needed a crewmember on set that was a licensed dive master.

I was happy to be a part of a feature film. Especially since my work with COPS was over for the season, and I knew I needed to find new work. What great timing!

The Punisher was an amazing experience for me, because it was the first major motion picture I would be able to work on. This film offered huge equipment trucks, catering, a massive budget, and the ability to close off city blocks just to shoot. It also starred John Travolta, Roy Scheider, and Thomas Jane! Yeah, this was big time for me. I had worked on many small budget feature films, but as I said, this would be the first real feature film for me. We were working in Fort DeSoto, which is a beautiful beach in St. Petersburg, Florida. Several of the scenes on this beach were supposed to emulate Puerto Rico in the story. Being part of the marine unit, I was able to work around all of the really cool scenes, like blowing up a boat, and even a fishing dock.

This was my first time working around pyrotechnics, and it was really interesting to see the world these crazy people live in. The first shot I would be a part of was supposed to be of a couple of the bad guys going down to the water, where a Donzi speed boat is at the edge of the water, full of money. They are on the boat making sure the stacks of money are secure, before they take off, only to find a hand grenade lying down in the hull. As they notice the bomb, they dive off as the boat blows up. If you have watched it in the movie, it is a great scene and looks really real!

How this shot was set up, was the boat was actually a Donzi that had been towed in, but it was just a hull. They had removed all of the inside interior, cables, motor, gas lines and everything. So it was really just a floating, non-usable, scrap yard boat hull, with a fresh paint job and some accessories to make it look usable. The boat had been set up with plastic explosives (C-4), and wired to a remote trigger up on the hill. Several cameras were all set up around the boat, and each one had a remote trigger to start the camera, so the operators would be out of harm's way. Each camera had a clear Plexiglas shield in front of it, to protect the camera and lens.

The marine unit's job was to place a floating absorption pad around the entire perimeter of the boat in the water, about ten yards out. This floating maxi pad was placed to absorb any oil or fuel that could possibly go into the ocean and hurt the fish. Even though no fuel or oil lines were on the boat, it was a mandatory requirement with the EPA, and they had officials on set to make sure we followed protocol. It's similar to having PETA on set when working with animals.

Once the explosion was finished, it would be the marine unit's job to jump into the water, and slowly bring the floating absorption pad back in, so it will retrieve any debris in the water. We had several of our crew ready to dive in and grab the pad after the explosion. The cool thing to me was the production team made everyone leave the beach, and go up the hill about thirty yards for safety reasons, except for us. Since we had to jump right in the water after the shot, we had an amazing view of the explosion, as we were hiding behind a sand dune only about ten yards away.

Safety is always priority one, and this production was incredibly safe. They really followed all protocol to make sure no matter what the shot was, that crew and talent came first. Once everything was in place, we started the countdown. We only had one Donzi, so that meant we only had one chance to get this shot. We also had to wait for the sun to go down just enough that the flames and explosion would look amazing on camera, so the timing was critical. Once everything had a green light, the countdown started. 5… 4… 3… 2… 1…. BOOM!

A HUGE plume of flames and explosion! The plume went about fifty feet straight up into the dark sky, and not only did it look amazing to my eye, you could feel the intense heat flow across us. The boat did explode, but not too badly. The explosives were packed to create more of a visual fire effect, and less of an actual blowout effect, so most of the boat hull stayed intact. But you could never tell that from the footage. As soon as we received the loudspeaker clear to enter the water, we ran in and started retrieving the floating maxi pad. We slowly brought it in, the EPA was happy, the director was happy, and the talent was safe. Just another good day in the field.

Unfortunately for me, I was only able to work a couple of weeks on The Punisher. I had fallen to really bad back pain, and my MRI had come back in, and I had to have a scheduled surgery. I did work until the day I had to leave for surgery, and was able to be a part of some amazing shots, and see some really cool things, like the dock explosion. The only sad thing for me was that I knew I was being hired as a day player, meaning they only needed me for the couple of weeks they were doing the water scenes, so I did not work the entire film. Because of that, I never received a credit in the film, but my experience was amazing! Even more importantly, my surgery went very well.

Blowdown
Kennedy Space Center

After The Punisher and my back surgery, I was eventually back to work. Once mobile again, I was doing smaller projects with Cliff and Curtis, but nothing major. I was just shooting or gripping for First Unit, but it did give me some quality time to spend with Kasen, my young son. After a couple of months, Bill Mills called me, and asked if I was available to work with him on a new show called Blowdown. This was a series that had been filmed for a while, but the production company, Parallax, is based out of Canada. Apparently, they could not get work permits to shoot in certain parts of the USA, so they sometimes had to hire a local crew to shoot this show. This time, it was mainly because they wanted to shoot in a military controlled airspace, Cape Canaveral Air Force Base, and the government would not give them permission, for national security reasons. Bill got the call, because he is known for these types of shoots, and had contacts that pursued him, so he hired me to work with him.

The premise was that one of the rocket towers, MST 40 (Mobile Service Tower), was to be removed strategically, and they had hired Controlled Demolition Incorporated to handle this task. This company has removed many large structures in the past, and we would be documenting how they decide to drop this structure in a complex way. The concept was to place shape charges in specific areas of the tower to drop it exactly where it needed to go.

The reason CDI was employed to drop the structure is because the rocket tower itself was located on Space Launch Complex 40. The reason it was called a mobile service tower was because it was just that, mobile. This structure had some pretty serious history, as it was the rocket launch tower for over fifty-five missions. It weighed 13.2 million pounds, and stood about two hundred feet tall. The 30-story high launch tower rested on four sets of extremely large railroad wheels, and sat on actual railroad track, going from the main launch headquarters, to the actual launch pad about a mile away. The launch pad itself was at the end of the track. Cape Canaveral Air Force Launch Station 40 was just one of several launch pads located within the Cape Canaveral complex. This launch pad was used for the Titan III and Titan IV launches between 1965 and 2005.

Space Exploration Technologies, or SpaceX, was leasing this launch pad for their new Falcon 9 rockets. They signed the lease in 2007 for the several launch pads they were going to acquire, and now this pad was on the docket. The MST was very old, and had poor structural integrity. But more importantly, the technology from 1965 was just not up to par with a new space company with new rockets. The tricky issue with leasing the launch pad, was the actual concrete pad was fine, but the tower itself had to be demolished. However, there were four lightning towers surrounding the launch tower that were still completely fine, and also cost about a couple million dollars each. These towers are surrounding all of the launch pads, and protect the rockets from lightning before and during a launch. Since Florida is more prone to lightning strikes than any other state, these are very necessary.

This massive structure had several floors and elevators, as well as staircases going up to the top. The main section inside the MST was a clean room that was probably 15 stories high in itself, and surrounded the rocket on three sides. To say the least, it was overwhelming to look at from the ground. My first thought was, "How in the hell are they going to make this thing go away?" It was like looking at a building downtown next to a bunch of other buildings.

We were staying at a hotel fairly close to the Space Center, so we were able to be there early every day to film the beginning of the demolition. After meeting all of the crew with CDI, the first thing that needed to be done, was to have the launch tower pulled all the way to the end of the pad to make sure it was ready to fall forward, and we shot all of this for the film. This process of actually rolling the tower to the end of the launch pad took most of the day, as it was being towed by cranes, and nothing like this goes quickly. Plus, it had not been moved in years, so it took some time to loosen up. The reason the tower needed to be at the end of the launch pad, was because at the end was a drop-down cavern. This drop down had a hole in the center, so when a rocket would take off, all of the flames from the rockets themselves would travel down this hole, and would be directed out of the cavern. They called this the Bat Cave, and it was also the perfect place for the tower to fall into after being demolished by explosives.

First, we shot the removal of the floor plates. One by one, using blow torches as cutting tools, they dropped to the floor. This slowly removed the bottom five floors of the structure. This needed to be done to lighten the structural integrity of the base of the tower, and by removing the majority of the steel inside the tower, it made the base much weaker.

They also removed most of the electrical conduit and wiring, as well as all of the air conditioning units, and just about anything of any significant weight. The first four days were just gutting the tower. A huge pile of steel and debris was tossed onto the ground, and another set of cranes and front-end loaders would pick up all of the debris, and haul it into trucks. The last couple of days were for wiring the tower to blow. A truck full of explosives showed up, and they all went to work placing shape charges into the structure. Mark, the owner of CDI, is amazing. He has the knowledge to tell his crews exactly where to put the shape charges, so the structure falls precisely where it needs to.

OK, full stop! Can you friggin' imagine a box truck full of high explosives driving down the road, and entering a military operated Air Force Base? Just saying! This in itself sounds crazy to me! Imagine the security clearance this truck must have had. Who was driving this truck? James Bond? It took me two weeks of background checks to get clearance to video this facility!

The process of getting the MST ready for demolition was very interesting to film. One crew would cut V shaped notches into the steel trusses supporting the tower, and another crew would place loaded shape charges into the V shaped hole, and then run detonation wire down the base of the tower. Bill and I both shot these technicians placing these high explosive charges into the steel truss of the structure. These were great shots of them placing high explosives into the beams. But what struck me as funny was watching these technicians after work, hitting the strip club next door to our hotel and getting trashed!

Every night the entire demo crew would go to the strip club and get hammered! God knows when they actually would get to bed each night. CDI did have a special crew for the explosive part of this, thank God. Once all of the explosives were in place, and all of the detonation cord was run the entire mile to the bunker at the other end of the complex, we were ready.

The last day, once everything was set, my job was to place a bunch of disposable cameras all around the tower. These are called lipstick cameras, as they are thin, long, and are mounted to wood plates. We had 100 foot cables attached to them, so we could put cameras literally right under the tower, and run the cable far enough away to connect them to record decks we had in tough plastic cases. Once everything was set, the countdown started. Bill was operating a high-speed camera about a mile away to capture the explosion in super slow motion. I was on a four-wheeler, called a Gator, and when everyone was a mile away in a safe zone, my job was to race over to each camera during the countdown and hit record on each deck. Then, I had to race over to the gate, where a driver was ready for me to jump in, and drive away before the tower blew up. The reason I had to do this at the last minute was because the batteries on the camera record deck only last about an hour, so they were to be the last thing powered up and set to record, so we would have plenty of time to capture the entire explosion. I am aware of the concept of collateral damage, so I just had to giggle and assume the reason I was chosen for this task was because of my vast knowledge of pushing the record button, as opposed to the other option.

This was a bit hairy for me, since I was the only person still left right next to an incredibly mammoth structure rigged with thousands of pounds of high explosives. If anything went wrong, or the timer screwed up and it blew up early, then I would for sure be many, many small pieces of Sean Michael Davis parts. I remember I had a radio, and was just waiting on the four-wheeler, until I heard Bill tell me to go ahead and start recording. Once I got that radio approval, I gunned the Gator! Gator racing was never a sport of mine but that day I could have won a friggin' race for sure!

Each record deck I got to was a race! I would jump off the Gator, run over to the deck, and hit the record button. This also needed to be done while making sure I did not run over the detonation cord stretched all over the structure, as that would also be bad. Then off to the next, one by one. Every time I jumped off that Gator, I was just waiting to hear the explosion early, knowing I was a goner!

Fortunately, I was able to get all of the decks recording and raced over to the gate. My heart rate was insane I'm sure! I jumped in the truck, and headed over to the safe zone to meet up with Bill and the guys. We all watched in amazement as the countdown came to an end, and in seconds, this entire behemoth of a tower went falling to the ground in a huge plume of grey smoke and debris. What made this so awesome, was the way the shape charges went off in a programmed sequence. First the 3rd floor run, and milliseconds later, half of the 5th floor went off. You could not notice this with the human eye, it just looked like a big explosion. But when we watch the slow-motion video, you could see each individual charges go off, and how the structure basically fell onto itself, allowing the launch tower to fall forward directly into the bat cave. It was such a cool sight to watch with your own eyes, and everyone was cheering and high fiving.

After we received the all clear from the Cape Canaveral safety team, we all rode back to ground zero to inspect the damage of the structure. The MST launch tower had fallen precisely where it was supposed to, with the majority of the structure now lying in a pile of steel rubble at the bottom of the bat cave. The lightning towers were perfectly intact, and now they would just have to slowly remove the rubble, and prepare this site for SpaceX.

When we wrapped all of our gear, we said goodbye to this amazing crew of talented explosive technicians, and headed back to our normal dull lives, LOL. Bill and I still talk about that adventure. If you would like to watch the show, just Google "Blow Down Rocket Tower"

Rhino Studios

After the back surgery, I worked on a bunch of local commercials and small projects with Curtis and Bill, as well as my own stuff. My friend Cliff came to me one day, and said, "Hey! Let's open a studio!" Cliff had dabbled in real estate for years, and him and his friend Tom owned a title agency, so getting properties is second nature to them. I told him I would love to, but money was tight, and I could not afford to pay another rent payment for a building. Cliff, as usual, had an answer. Other people's money! His business partner, Tom, had a friend named Paul, and Paul owned his own real estate maintenance company, as well as some rental units.

Paul had recently lost his wife due to an illness, and was interested in finding something to do with his time to keep his mind occupied, for obvious reasons. What better way to do it than hanging out with a couple of friendly but crazy filmmakers? I really liked Paul from the moment I met him. Paul is a talented craftsman in his trade, but more importantly, he is a really good person.

So, Cliff found an old building in downtown St. Pete that had high ceilings and big rooms. The rent was pretty cheap, as it needed a lot of renovations. Next thing you know, we were meeting with the landlord, and signing a lease. I was a bit nervous about taking on another project, but Cliff felt pretty confident that it would all be okay, so we signed the lease and started the build out. I learned something else about Cliff, he was very handy, and created some really cool elements for the building. He put a bar in the front room, and designed a large mountain next to the front doorway, with a reproduction of the Hollywood Sign on it. He even ran Christmas lights so it so would look glittery when the ceiling lights were off. He purchased aluminum siding and made that the bar structure, and then just placed a simple wood bar top across it. The bar looked really cool. Meanwhile, Paul was building an amazing CYC wall (this is a "no seam" backdrop, rounded at the corners), and also wiring the electric in the ceiling for the lights. The construction, paint, drywall, and lights took about a month. I had a garage full of equipment and lights, and we used these lights and gear to set up the studio, and got it all working pretty quickly. When we were nearly finished, we had our grand opening event. Cliff was able to get the pizza guy across the street to donate pizzas for the event. We had wine and beer, and a had wonderful turnout.

Everyone posted on social media about our grand opening, and we told everyone we knew about this event. I was really proud of the studio, and proud that my mom was able to show up for our grand opening event, and be a part of my future success. Rhino was a blast, and we shot some really fun stuff while we were there. The studio lasted about three years, until we all decided we just were not making any money, and it was starting to cost us way more than what we were bringing in. I had gone back to COPS, so I was not there to help, and people were not renting, as it was just a slow time for production. Eventually, the landowner decided he wanted to do something totally different with the building, and removed us from the lease, and we just moved out and moved on. I will tell you, owning a studio is like owning a boat, the first day and the last day are most definitely your favorite days. Everyone wants one, but the upkeep and maintenance, and the hassle, is so overwhelming. If you're not making money with it, then shut it down. You can have a green screen in your garage, and do just as well.

Skyway Down
12-04-08

Skyway Down was a pivotal project for me. I had no idea what this moment would become, and to this day, I am so grateful for making the film, yet still so sad. When certain things happen in our lives that we never expected, we might think we are prepared, but usually we are not. While I was shooting the TV show COPS, we were living in St. Petersburg, Florida. My wife and I had just had our son, and everything was fine, until we had some bad people decide to sneak in the backyard fence one day. They were probably trying to break into our house. My wife was at home taking care of our newborn child, when she walked across the back part of the house to see two scary faces staring into the back French door windows! So, of course, she screamed and yelled at them! As they were probably just as surprised to see her inside the house screaming at them, they turned around and slowly walked away down the back alley. It's common for criminals to rob houses during the day, because that is usually when homeowners are at work.

This was not uncommon in this neighborhood, but when you have a newborn child, I understood my wife's concerns. So, she called me after the fact with serious frustration in her voice, letting me know that this shit was not going to happen again, and she wanted to live in a safer place pronto.

My response was, as it should have been, "Well, if you can find a place then we can move as soon as I get back home."

I was at this time in Los Angeles shooting COPS, and I had zero control over whatever was going on in St. Petersburg, Florida. I wanted her to feel safe, of course, especially with a newborn child, but I could not have been farther away if I tried. So, I just told her to start looking for a new home, and when I was done with this venue, we would pack up and move to wherever she wanted to go.

The next day, Lara started looking for a new home for us. I remember when she called me before I was heading out to roll call at the sheriff's office, and told me she had found a place in Manatee County across the bridge, called Sneed Island. It sounded like a lovely little place, and we could afford it. So I told her to put down the deposit and work out the deal, and we would move as soon as I got back in town.

After the last week of shooting, I flew back home, and she told me all about the new house she had rented, then we packed up and started the move. At the time, I still had the camera truck, so we loaded it up with furniture, and I started making drives across the Skyway Bridge into our new county and new home.

It was a wonderful little place on the island, and I was really happy with the choice she had made for our new home. I would make multiple trips across the bridge during those several days of bringing our stuff from one home to another, and everything seemed to be working well with the transition. I never even thought about the drive over the Skyway Bridge, other than how beautiful it was, until that fateful day.

I'm sure I had made that trip across the bridge five or six times, transferring our stuff to our new home, before fate slapped me in the face. I remember driving up to the top of the bridge, on a beautiful day with a clear sky. This was the kind of bridge that when you get to the top, you just realize how scenic everything around you is. The sky, the cables, the view, the boats down below, this is what makes Florida such an amazing place to live. Then it happened. I looked over to the left, and there she was, a young lady. She had stretched one of her legs over the side and was straddled across the ledge.

I can only imagine what must have been going through her mind at that very moment, it must have been pain and suffering and sadness to get to that level. She was young, maybe in her late twenties or early thirties, with blonde hair, and wearing green plaid pants and a tan shirt. I pulled over to the emergency lane of my side of the bridge (the Skyway is actually two bridges running North and South), and dialed 911. As the call connected, and I heard a female voice say, "911, what is your emergency?", I watched this young lady lean over the wall, and fall to her death.

I was frozen, as what I had just watched was so strange to me. Working on COPS, I had seen so many tragedies and sad things, yet this seemed so very surreal to me. It just happened right in front of my eyes, and yet I had no response that would help.

There was nothing I could do to keep this young lady from falling two hundred feet to her death right in front of me! She made a choice, and I was a part of her choice just by being there to witness this, but helpless to help her in any way. One moment, she was straddled over the wall, and then she was gone. During those seconds of realizing she had just leaned over and made the choice to end her life, she was actually falling two hundred feet to her demise, and no one else on the planet could change her decision.

I told the 911 dispatcher that I had just watched a young lady jump off the Skyway Bridge, and after a brief pause, the dispatcher said, "Please hold." Then, after what seemed like an eternity, another woman clicked on the line, and again said, "911, what's your emergency?" This really seemed strange, but again, I told her I just watched someone jump off of the Skyway Bridge. She responded and told me that she had a couple other calls that had come in, and they were dispatching an officer to the scene. After I hung up, I really had no idea what to do. I was on the other side of the bridge, and did not want to get out of my truck because of all of the fast-moving cars driving by, and the signs posted saying it was illegal to pull over at the top of the bridge, unless you were having car trouble. I was pulled over, so I put the truck in gear and started driving down the bridge, knowing that I had done everything I could possibly do. I decided I would head to the new house to unload, and possibly make one more trip before it got too dark.

This event stuck in my mind the entire trip to the new house. I just watched a young girl commit suicide.

So many emotions went scrolling through my mind, so many thoughts about this stranger, and what she had just done, and what she must have been going through. What could I have done differently? Or better? Or how could I have possibly kept her from jumping? By maybe trying to talk to her? I know she never would have heard me, because I was so far away. Trust me, if you are ever in this situation, you will question every second after the fact, and then you will question yourself again and again.

I had seen many suicides after the fact because of COPS. I can remember several calls we went on where we entered a home to find a man, or a woman, dead from their own hand in many fashions. The most grotesque, I must say, had to be hangings. Gunshots, of course, are very bloody and messy, but hangings just leave a macabre lingering visual that is hard to remove. The body is lifeless, but the skin does a thing called marbling, which is due to the lack of oxygen. It loses the tan color, and turns white and blue, and kind of has dots all over it, or streaks like a steak. Usually the eyes roll back up in the head, and sometimes the bladder releases as well. So, you can only imagine what this end of life looks like for the police who are called on to check on someone, when family or friends are concerned. I had, unfortunately, witnessed this many times. So my point is, I was kind of numb to suicide as a whole, because it had become normal to me as a cameraman, and I had also become kind of cynical, because of my past with COPS.

Well, this situation had me in a bit of a dilemma. I could not stop thinking about what had happened.

In the past, during my venues, I could just shut off some of the things I had witnessed once I got back to the hotel, but this was different. This was the first thing on my mind all night long. I could not shut it off. It just kept popping right back up. Who was this girl? Why was her life so horrible that this was the best option? Did her mom even yet know she was gone? Her family? Did she have a husband or kids? So many thoughts crossed my mind during that drive to our new house, our new life with our newborn son, our new home of happiness, white picket fences, puppies, and friendly neighbors.

After dropping off the furniture to our new home, I decided to not make another run, and just try to detach from what I had witnessed. I just worked around the new house, setting up the couch and loveseat, and little things I had on the truck. Lara eventually came home from work, and by this point we were living in the new house, so we poured a glass of wine and sat on the back patio to discuss the day. I told her of the events I had witnessed, and also told her how much it had affected me. I wanted to do something about it, but was not sure what to do. We discussed everything that happened, and it finally hit me. I needed to make a film about the bridge, and about suicide, and hopefully it could help someone down the road. I had the equipment, the knowledge, and the means to make a film. I just had no idea about suicide, nor how I would start or end this film. I had a new mission, and I was going to make this film. That was the beginning of my new venture, and my new goal to possibly help deter the next sad soul who might consider jumping of that bridge.

Education
Learning to Edit

Once I had decided to focus my attention to this project, the first thing I had to do was educate myself on the bridge, the suicide jumpers, and the history behind the bridge. Of course, the first step was to get online and Google the bridge. I learned so much so quickly, it floored me. I learned that in 1980 the bridge collapsed due to a freighter crashing into the support beams during a bad storm because of bad visibility. When the bridge collapsed, several cars went into the water, including a Greyhound bus. Thirty-three people died because of this horrible collision, and the bridge had to be rebuilt. I also learned that this bridge had been used for suicide from the day it was erected back in the fifties. Back then, there was no way of documenting how many people jumped, so it was just a myth as to how many souls had ended their lives from the bridge.

After that search, I also found a website that was all about the Skyway Bridge and the jumpers. This website was so incredibly important to my research, as it had documentation of jumpers for so many years in the past. It also had blogs and posts from family members and friends, as well as drive-bys, and people just interested in the "romanticism" of the bridge and the fatalities it had taken over the years. People would leave comments on this site, some were nasty, some friendly, and some just plain confusing. Nevertheless, this website was such an incredible resource for me to educate myself about this bridge and the suicides.

After a couple of days of searching the web, I found the name of the young girl who had jumped that day. I saw a photo of her with her name, and I found her Facebook page still active. I saw her so clearly, and it was most definitely the girl I saw climbing over the small three foot wall and leaning over to end her life. It was such a strange feeling to see her face again, and all of her Facebook photos with her smiling and posing with friends, now knowing that she was no longer a part of this world. I researched as much as I could, and took notes on the bridge and all the data I had acquired from the websites. Then, I started my initial process of how was I going to make this documentary.

I knew I could shoot the interviews and scenic footage, but I had never edited anything before. I made some calls to local editors who I had worked with in the past, and scheduled appointments to meet, and see if they would be receptive to putting my footage together once I had it. One local editor was interested, so I met with her and told her my plan. I wanted to start shooting interviews and extra content, and hopefully find a local voice talent to narrate the film with the best of intentions to deter future jumpers. She agreed to help me, because she felt my intentions for making the film were of merit. Of course, I had no money, so it would have to be done during her slow times. But hey, that was better than no editing, and I was not in a hurry, so great. The next step was to try to schedule interviews with family members of lost loved ones, and public officials who are involved with the technical aspects of a bridge jump. People like Recovery Divers, Law Enforcement, Medical Examiners, Highway Patrol, etc.

My first call was to the sheriff's office. Since I had worked with them on COPS, I was hoping for a positive response for my film, and I did get one. The sheriff said to give me anything I needed to help make the film happen. Then, I called the crisis center and made the same request, and they also offered me any of their resources to help make the film.

So I started scheduling interviews with anyone who would be willing to sit down with me. Again, I had zero knowledge of suicide or mental issues, so I was learning as I went. My first interview was from contacting the website that had all of the Skyway Bridge suicides on it. I had left a request for the webmaster to please post a note that a local filmmaker wanted to interview anyone who had a relationship with someone who had jumped from the bridge, and would be willing to sit down on camera and tell their story. I had a response within a few weeks of the post. Her name was Terri Smith, and her brother had jumped a couple of years prior, and she was still grieving from the loss. I'm sure I was as uncomfortable as she was. I had my gear, but really no idea how this interview would go. I met with her, and then set up my camera and a couple of small lights. I was going to have her sit on the couch in her living room. So I put a lavalier (wireless mic) on her, and also placed a boom pole overhead, so I had two clean channels of audio. I had not really done a lot of sound work in the past, but it was just me and her, and I knew I had to make sure everything was working as good as it could, as I would not get a second chance if I had an equipment failure.

This was a great test for me, and luckily, this interview went extremely well. Terri was comfortable, and was ready to give a great on camera interview. I think I was actually more nervous than she was. Terri was ready to talk and tell her story. She wanted this film to be made, and she wanted to get the word out. At the time, I was the only one interested in helping her with that. Most of the media organizations did not want to take on this complex issue. Once we were set, and the lights and camera and audio levels seemed good, I hit the record button and asked her to tell me her story. Her brother had jumped a couple years ago, and she had so many unanswered questions. She was so captivating, and amazing on camera. She really did an amazing job, and I knew at that moment that I could never stop until the film was finished. It just had to be made. Too many passionate people were involved in this issue, and something had to be done.

I left her house with a couple of tapes of great stuff and a happy heart. I felt I was on my way to possibly making a great film and a significant difference. I had no idea how long this task would take, but I knew I had a great first interview, and was excited for the next one. If only I knew then what I know now, I would have still made the film, but would have been way better prepared. I scheduled several more interviews, and shot a lot of scenic footage of the bridge to compile my footage.

As I said, an acquaintance of mine had offered to edit the film for me when I first started, because she believed in the cause. So after I had acquired a ton of footage, 14 tapes so far, I went to her faculty to drop off the first batch. She looked at the box of tapes, and then told me, "Sorry, Sean. I just really don't have the time to edit this for you."

I was taken aback a bit, as this was not part of the plan. I had shot for years but had never edited anything. I had no idea what to do other than try to find another editor. I went back on with COPS a week later. While I unpacked my suitcase in my hotel room, some of the crew came over to say hello, and my sound guy Carlos showed up. I told him about my conundrum with my editor when he asked me how the film was going, and he said, "I have a copy of

Final Cut Pro, it's an editing program, and I can give you a copy of it."

I thought, what the hell? I can do it myself. I just need to learn how to edit, and that will not keep me from finishing this project. So I took him up on the offer, and started learning the software at night after we would get back to the hotel. Just like any new skill, this took a lot of time, and caused a lot of initial frustration by learning from simple mistakes like, SAVE YOUR PROJECT OFTEN!

I lost several initial timelines because I did not save my project, but fool me once... After the two-month venue with COPS, I had learned enough to start really putting the project together with a small amount of confidence. I borrowed playback decks from my friends to import the tapes I had shot, and started to catalog the footage, so I knew what I had and where it would be in the system. Originally, I was going to have a friend of mine, Ted Webb, who is a local radio personality, narrate the film. He has a great voice and very well known in town, and he said he would be happy to do it. So I wrote some copy, met him at the radio station, and had him read the copy and email it to me.

I was trying to work his narration in, but as I was importing interview clips into the timeline, I was really having trouble finding spots to insert his narrative. The show was really working and flowing without a narration, so I decided to just let the interviews flow into the next interview. Several times, I would have a clip of one person asking a question about the bridge, or the system in place to deal with a jumper situation, and then I would be able to cross fade to another person explaining how their part of the system worked, and how they help.

It actually flowed very well this way, so Ted was now off the hook, and I could start moving forward with a plan for keeping the film going. Some of the interviews just did not work well in the timeline, others worked incredibly well, and I had a good amount of footage to create a strong opening. As time went on, and I had a good start to the film, I still had to work and pay bills, so it was just a matter of juggling paying work with non-paying documentary work. A good film takes time, and this film was no exception. Sometimes I would go a month or two without any forward movement, because I was working, or I was not getting emails for new interviews. But patience is a virtue, and I have a lot of patience.

About a year into the film, I received an email from my friend Bob Hite. Bob was a retired lead news anchor for News Channel 8, and he had received word that I was making a film about the bridge. Bob is a boat captain by hobby, and would focus on many nautical news clips when he was an anchor. He loved the water and anything to do with Tampa Bay, so he asked me if I would like to use his original footage of when the bridge collapsed. OMG! Are you kidding me? YES! This would be an amazing addition to my film. Now I have a history of the bridge, as well as being able to incorporate this into my film. I gratefully accepted, and he sent me a DVD to import into my system.

The Sunshine Skyway Bridge was built in 1954 to allow easy access from Sarasota to St. Petersburg, Florida. It is over fourteen miles long, and is considered one of the longest bridges in the world. It also, unfortunately, has a history as a destination for people to jump from, and has developed a stigma because of this. Stories have been told of people driving over the top and seeing ghosts, or visions of a lady in a white dress standing on the edge. There are also stories of people being forced to jump by the mafia.

A real history moment that was just as tragic happened in 1980. In really bad weather with horrible visibility, a freighter ran into one of the support beams of the bridge, causing it to collapse, sending a Greyhound bus full of people into the water, killing all of them. A couple other cars went in also, one of them actually landed on the freighter, saving the driver. The boat captain issued a mayday call, and recovery divers were sent out to recover the bodies. The bridge was shut down for a long time, so traffic had to use the other bridge right next to it for northbound and southbound traveling while they rebuilt a new bridge.

Since Bob was the lead anchor when this happened, he sent me awesome footage of him on camera explaining, "Today we have witnessed the worst nautical tragedy in Tampa Bay history."

This was great footage, and I was so thrilled to have it, that it actually became the opener of the film. Why not show a major historical event about the bridge, and then go into the stigma of the bridge regarding suicide jumpers? Things were looking up for my project, and I was really starting to get happy with how it was progressing. I realized it was a blessing that no one else was editing the film, because it was my vision, and that vision can so easily get lost when someone else gets involved.

During my time working shows and spending time with the family, I was working on the film. It was coming along well. I had interviewed recovery divers, highway patrol troopers, and family members who had lost loved ones to the bridge. One of the best contacts I made while shooting the film was Steve Gaskins. He was the Public Information Officer for the Tampa office of the Florida Highway Patrol, and he was willing to meet with me, and take me up to the top of the bridge to get shots that normally you cannot get. It is actually illegal to stop at the top of the bridge and do anything. If a car stops at the top of the bridge, the cameras notice it, and that goes back to the dispatchers as a possible jumper, so they contact the troopers. That is not a good thing if you are just taking pictures. So, Steve and I met and rolled up to the top, where I was able to really get some nice shots of the emergency phones, the wall, and everything else.

Steve has worked with the FHP for many years, and he is really calm and collected and knowledgeable. When he realized that I was trying to help people, he really helped me in any way he could. He would send me statistics and anything I needed that he could offer to help me make the film. I stayed in contact with Steve, even after I was done with the film, and we have become good friends. Steve is a great trooper. I have worked with so many law enforcement officers over the years, and Steve is one of the best. I can honestly say I am happy that this film brought us together as friends. Fate works in strange ways.

One day, I received an email from a gentleman named Hanns Jones. Hanns had jumped from the bridge several years ago and survived, which is extremely rare. He was now very active in talking with anyone who would listen, to keep them from making the same mistake. He agreed to an interview, and we met at a local park in downtown St. Pete.

The most difficult part of making a film by yourself is making sure everything is working correctly on the technical level. This was a very important interview for me to get, so I did not want to make any mistakes that day. I set up a reflector board to give him a little more light on his face, put a wireless mic on him, and set up the camera framing it just right. I had headphones on, so I could listen to his levels, and once everything was set and seemed ok, I started the interview. I prompted Hanns by simply saying, "Tell me why you jumped, and tell me what went through your mind the second your feet left the top of the bridge." Hanns was amazing. He gave me so many insane audio bytes for the film, and his whole goal was to offer counsel to anyone who would even consider this as an option to end their life. He had basically been destroyed by the fall, or more accurately, the landing. He broke his neck, ruptured both of his lungs, broke his ribs, ruptured his pancreas, and broke his hip from the fall. He told me it was like having someone tie you to a truck and a tree, and drive off. "It rips people apart," he said.

"The romanticism of the bridge," he added, "is an illusion!" I could not have said it better! The hair rose on the back of my neck as he was talking. I drove home just hoping to God that this tape was all good, and that I had good audio and exposure. I HAD to use this footage. I was so excited for the film. Sometimes, you just don't know until you upload the footage into the computer, and really look and listen to it. I think I even drove more carefully than normal, not to keep me safe, but the tapes! LOL. This footage was great, and it would definitely be a huge part of the film.

The top of the bridge is two hundred feet high, and normally when someone jumps into water from this height, it is like hitting concrete. That's why most people die, not from drowning, although that is what eventually happens, but from the blunt force trauma created during the landing. Hanns was just very lucky to live, but most are not. I realized this even more when I interviewed the Tampa medical examiner. They showed me how bad the body is smashed up when it hits the water, and they gave me coroner reports of past jumpers. Reading the amount of damage people sustained when they hit the water was eye opening for me. This was another great interview, and I was really on a roll getting some great footage and information.

Another great opportunity happened again by chance, as one day I was just strolling through my local music store looking at guitars, and the salesperson and I started chatting. Somehow, I started talking about my documentary, and he told me he had just moved to Florida from Los Angeles, and he was a music composer for feature films! Are ya kidding me? He agreed to score my film for free, so he could get his name out locally! So, while I was finishing up bits of the film, he was scoring it at his house, and then would just email me the sound bits to add to my timeline. It worked flawlessly!

The COPS season had ended for the year, and I was now unemployed again. A strange thing to grasp with this type of career is, unlike a normal nine to five job with benefits, you'll have a good thing going, but when it ends, you are looking at your calendar asking, "What's next?" That's a scary position to be in when the bank account is low. The bills don't stop coming in just because the work is over.

Fortunately, Curtis called me, and asked if I would be available to work with him on a low budget film he would be directing, called The Glass Window. The film was being produced by Ray Romano's brother, and it was about a cop who finds religion. Curtis does a lot of faith-based films, as he is also a believer, and he really enjoys working on these types of shows. This film would be shot with his RED camera, and had a good enough budget to really make a nice film. I had a lot of fun working on it, even though we only worked a month or so shooting it. Hey, it's a paycheck, and I was able to be surrounded by friends and family while working on it.

After Curtis's film ended, I had a couple more calls for small gigs. Meanwhile, I was really able to assemble the majority of Skyway Down. I interviewed the sheriff, and some of his high-profile deputies, as well as some other family members of jumpers, and had compiled enough footage to finish the film. So after several months of editing at night after the family was asleep, I had a finished film. Yes, I continued to make changes and fine tune the film, but the bones were in place, and I was really happy with what I had done.

Some of my friends helped me design a cover, and I sent it off to a printer to print, copy, and shrink-wrap my first set of DVDs! What an exciting day when that box came to the door, and I opened it to see my film! It looked amazing. My heart was so happy with the accomplishment I had made, not just for myself, but also hopefully for society.

The Tampa Bay Times got word of what I was doing, and they asked to interview me about my documentary. That was exciting because this would offer me more exposure to help get the film out, so I did the interview. Then I met with the sheriff's office after I had my first box of DVDs produced, and gave them fifty DVDs to put on their shelf and sell, so that all proceeds would go to the

Fallen Officers Foundation. Honestly, my heart was on fire with happiness, because I really felt what I was doing was good and right.

I also entered Skyway Down into the Sunscreen Film Festival, because why not? I spent three years on it, and it would allow more local people to see it, and at least talk about it. I hoped everyone would like it, since I did get some pretty shitty emails while making it, including one death threat! Not everyone was positively receptive to me diving into a topic that is quite painful. Many family members were afraid I would disparage their loved one's name. Occasionally I would receive a really less than friendly email. This is just part of the deal, and I would try to respond as kind as I could, or sometimes just not respond at all.

The film, and the exposure I received while making the film, was pretty awesome. I think it helped me get a little more credibility in town, and more importantly, I believe the people who watched it told other people to watch it. That is how you get a film like this to the world. It also helped more local companies recognize me as a filmmaker.

The most amazing thing that happened was after I was done, and had moved on from the documentary, I was invited to the Sunscreen Film Festival because they had accepted the film! This was an exciting time for me, but also scary, because I was concerned about how people would receive such a film. Normally, the film festivals play films that are artsy, or look like French films, with cinematic camera angles and amazing lighting techniques. My film had none of this. My film was raw, gritty, and real. I borrowed any camera I could get, and most of it was shot in basic standard definition, as opposed to a high definition the fancy expensive cameras shoot in. I did not have a fancy expensive system, or any other camera that would make it look better.

I did show up, and had a little booth with a backdrop, thanks to my friends who made me a poster of the front

DVD cover, and tried to get people to watch the film. I put on a jacket and tie, and asked people to watch my film, just like the 30 or 40 other people that night promoting their films. The theater was packed when my film played, and I felt the response was great! After the documentary was finished, I was asked to stand in front of the audience, and explain my purpose for the film. This was a bit uncomfortable for sure, as I have never really been good at speaking in front of a theater full of people. But this is all part of the film premier experience, I guess. I had some experience with this from past short films Cliff and I had submitted, but this was my first time presenting my own baby, and I was so proud. It really did make this an exciting time for me. At the end of the day, I was just truly hoping the film would get enough exposure to possibly help someone in need.

My mom knew I was going to the awards ceremony, and wanted to be there with me, as Lara was at home watching our son. I just knew I was not going to win any awards, as I was being placed with the other local filmmakers who had premiered some amazing films. This included Curtis's film, The Glass Window, which we had shot with beautiful cameras and amazing lighting. There were a couple other films I knew were awesome as well, so I wanted to show my face out of respect for the other filmmakers, and then get back home at a reasonable hour. I was beside myself when the man behind the podium said that Skyway Down had won Best Florida Film! Holy crap! Really? My film was elected the Best Florida Film? What an amazing night, and what a wonderful accomplishment. I was so proud, but also sad that my family was not there to witness this night. I was so convinced that I would never win, I had told them not to go.

I believe the film is amazing, and my heart tells me it's worth all the time invested. Anyone in pain should watch it, whether it helps or not, so at least you can get the information or help needed today. When the Tampa Bay Times had interviewed me about the film, I had told them if I could save just one life, then all of my efforts would be worth it. I truly feel this documentary has helped some people in need, and that is the reason I wanted to make it. Skyway Down is on YouTube, please watch it.

Dolphin Tale: 2011

In early 2011, Rico Browning called me again to work on a new film called Dolphin Tale. It would be a story about Winter the dolphin, who had his tail cut off because he was trapped in netting rope from a fisherman's boat. Rico asked me to work with him on the film, again for insurance purposes, as they needed a divemaster to be part of the marine safety crew. Plus, he was happy with the work I had done with him on The Punisher, and we had developed a friendship. I would be a day player, similar to when I worked on The Punisher, but this worked out great since I had so many other things going on at the time. I think I worked about twenty days total on the film, mostly at Clearwater Aquarium. Working on features is such a different experience from working on television shows. Features have huge budgets, and much more equipment. The parking lots are filled with semi-trucks full of gear. They have full-service food trucks, camera, grip, and electric trucks, plus full size generators and camera crane rigs. It's pretty insane to see how much goes into a feature film, and just like The Punisher, it was pretty amazing.

The benefit of being hired to work on a feature film is you are guaranteed months of consistent work, but the downfall is the actual day rates are significantly lower. It's actually an hourly rate, and you really do not make a decent wage unless you go into a lot of overtime. This usually happens, but then you are exhausted, and you have to be back to work seven hours later to do it all over again.

I was able to work with the main cast, and I have to say, they were all a real pleasure to work with. Morgan Freeman, Ashley Judd, Harry Connick Jr., and Chris Christopherson were all such kind and friendly people to work with. It was neat to be able to say I worked on this film, and when I watched it in the theaters, it was even more fun to know I had a part in it. My son, Kasen, loved the film! Thanks again, Rico!!!

An Amazing Opportunity!

Every once in a while you receive a call for a once in a lifetime opportunity. This happened back in October of 2013, from a friend of mine, Kerry Buck. Kerry is a local shooter, and his brother is Chris Buck, who shoots House Hunters. Chris and Kerry are brothers, but they do the same thing as a career, and have two separate companies as director of photography shooting shows. You might think this would create some arguments from time to time bidding on shows, but they are brothers and love each other, so somehow, they make it work.

They are both very talented directors of photography, and this time Kerry called to ask me if I could cover a shoot for him. It was kind of a last-minute notice, but he had just booked a three week long gig, so he asked me if I could cover him on his other gig shooting for the Weather

Channel at MacDill Air Force Base. I was available, so I told him I would be happy to. He told me it would be a very long day because of the travel involved, but would be an exciting shoot. I had to fill out some paperwork and send it in ASAP, as not just anyone can get access into MacDill, since it is Central Command Center for the United States in times of war. We had just three days to get everything submitted and processed, but the paperwork all went through just fine. I showed up, and was directed by armed guards holding M16 assault rifles to the NOAA air hanger. NOAA stands for the National Oceanic Atmospheric Association, and their job is to monitor all aspects of the weather across the world. They have eight planes of all different sizes that fly to foreign countries for weather-related issues.

Two of the planes are Hurricane Hunter P-3s, and our job that today was to take one of the planes, and fly into a hurricane that was way out in the Gulf of Mexico. This was why the Weather Channel had employed a Tampa Bay shooter to capture the crew taking samples and monitoring data during this hurricane. I know a lot of the local shooters would have turned this gig down, because it is dangerous, and to say the least, a bit of a bumpy ride. But I was a tough guy cameraman that had shot for COPS, so this would be a walk in the park. Or, that's what I thought. The P-3 is a large plane, similar to a Boeing 700 commercial airline, but is gutted inside and built sturdily enough to fly directly into the insane winds of a hurricane. The inside passenger compartment was set up with rows of computer desks, each one with a different purpose for monitoring information and data relating to wind and temperature. In the past, the P-3 was used for monitoring submarine activity during the Cold War.

I showed up very early, and drove to Hanger 5, then met with the main crew chief for NOAA, and we went over the details for this mission. I grabbed the camera and shot some pre-interview stuff, as well as a bunch of B-roll of them prepping for the flight. We had to board and takeoff early because of the amount of flight time it would take just to get to the hurricane, and we wanted daylight conditions when we got there.

What made this event even more interesting, was the day of shooting was during a government furlough, which meant a lot of government agencies were shut down because of budget cuts. This also meant NOAA had been shut down for several days, with more to come, except for this mission. You don't get to schedule a major hurricane. This hurricane put one of the two planes back in temporary service, so they could document the data, in case it came close to the United States and became an emergency.

We boarded the plane, and had to fly at 30,000 feet for seven hours just to get to the hurricane. Then they did data collection for about four hours, and then it was seven hours back home. So Kerry was right, this was going to make for a long friggin' day. I was able to plug the camera battery charger into an outlet in the rear next to the toilets, so I had plenty of charged batteries for the next eighteen hours. Kerry gave me a box of tapes, so I had plenty of tape stock to shoot a bunch of cool stuff. Now honestly, seven hours in a plane just to get to the hurricane is way too much footage to shoot. And then four hours of crazy, bumpy hurricane insertion footage is more than enough for what would wind up being maybe ten minutes of edited footage for the show. But I shot a lot, because I was really interested in the plane, and the people who do this, and I learned a lot about how they do what they do.

While we were flying over to the middle of nowhere, way south of Mexico, I went into the cockpit and shot some really cool footage of the pilots, and an intense dark tropical system swirling with anger over the middle of the ocean. The plane was nicknamed Kermit the Frog, and the other P-3 was called Miss Piggy. This one had a fluffy Kermit the Frog hanging from the middle of the cockpit. Once we got close, the captain told me to go back and have a seat, as it was about to get really rough.

I strapped myself in and placed the camera on my lap, as I figured I could still shoot from my seat once we got into the storm. I learned pretty quickly that was not going to happen, as what they do is basically fly a bow tie or criss cross through this insane weather system, and it throws this huge plane all over the place. I was not prepared for exactly how much we would fall from a high altitude to a low altitude in a matter of seconds, and then back up to God knows where. But after several minutes of trying to locate your stomach, you quickly realize that camera framing becomes less of a concern than keeping whatever you ate for lunch from obtaining a higher altitude than your throat.

These wonderful moments usually only lasted about five minutes, and then they would be out of the hurricane, but only so they could turn around and go back into the belly of the beast again. I learned I had about five minutes of vomit control, and then about three minutes of wiping the saliva off of my mouth and regaining my composure, before we went back into fun mode. Imagine doing this for four hours. What amazed me was all of the crew were so used to this, that they were all fine. They were dropping tubes with transmitters out of the plane through specialized shoots that would allow these tubes to fall down to the earth and land in the water, and then the transmitters would send data backup to the plane. This data would include water temperature, current, and barometric pressure readings. As we were flying through different parts of the hurricane, the crew was basically building a 3D layer of the hurricane based on the data transmitted back up to the plane.

Meanwhile, my sick ass was trying to put a camera on my shoulder, and shoot something other than my ingested cheeseburger, that was now 3 seats behind me. I would un-strap and run though the plane while we were in the calm moments, and try to get as much footage of the crew working on the computer desks that they were strapped into. Since this plane had rows and rows of computer stations, and each one had a specific task they were working on, I was trying to shoot each crewmember entering information, as well as others who were preparing the next set of tubes to drop out of the plane. Every once in a while, I would run up to the cockpit to shoot the pilots maneuvering the plane to get to the next level and position to fly back into the monster, then run back to my seat for the next roller coaster ride. Honestly, after about an hour of this, I was also comfortable enough to focus on my job and not my stomach. These technicians are amazing, and I gained so much respect for what they do, and the reason they do it. The information they are able to get back to the United States during a major hurricane can save lives, and that makes them true heroes risking their lives to save ours.

The shoot went well, and it also gave me enough time to really talk with some of the crew on the flight back home. The best part of this experience was, because of the furlough, we discussed all of the NOAA planes being grounded at MacDill. I was told this was the first time EVER that all of the NOAA planes were at the same hanger, at the same time. So I offered that if they would like, I could show up the next morning and take some amazing photographs of all of the planes at Hangar 5. This offer went over great, and even though they would have to get permission to get me back on the Air Force base grounds again, it would make sense, so why not?

They were able to get approval for this photo session while we were still in the air, and already had a plan before we landed. Once we finally landed and were back on stable ground, we discussed our next day photo shoot. Someone at MacDill would have a Condor ready (this is a lift machine to get us way high up off the ground), and would have already placed all of the planes correctly, and sprayed the ground with water to make the tarmac look really nice. They worked on this overnight, as I showed up very early, so we could get the sunrise light to make the shots even better. Honestly, everything worked like clockwork. The planes were placed perfectly, the ground looked nice and wet, and the lift was placed right in the middle of the planes. So, I was able to be lifted way up in the sky, and take a ton of photos. I also took a ton of creative photos of each plane individually, and emailed everything to them after color correcting and making some black and whites just for fun.

At the end of the day, experiences like this can pay off even though I did not get paid to do the photo shoot. I offered it, but I already had a great paying gig shooting the hurricane footage, and just being part of this experience was more than enough. But to be able to go back the next day to take pictures of some amazing planes in an amazing place, anyone would have done this for free. Right?

It truly was a once in a lifetime experience for everyone involved. I went home feeling high as a kite for what a crazy two days this had become. And to top it all off, a couple of months later, the crew leader emailed me with a release to sign. NOAA Washington, the main NOAA website, wanted to use my photography for their website. Are you kidding me? That's awesome! It would be the only time they had images of all of their planes on the ground, at the same time. Still no pay, but a credit would be issued on the bottom of a photograph that would be on a national website. How cool is that? Yes, definitely worth my time, and worth the experience, as I am writing about it now in my book because it was that cool. I don't really miss the roller coaster ride of the plane, and I can say now I don't think I would offer to shoot it again. But I'm truly glad I was able to experience it, and happy that this gig turned into a next day photo shoot that I can always be proud to be a part of.

Another really cool shoot that Kerry had put me on, was the Firestone Grand Prix of St. Petersburg. This was an annual event that occurs every year in St. Pete, where they close off the streets and have an IndyCar Series race. Since 2009, the race has served as the season opener for this sporting event. Our job was to document the Rahal tent, since Bobby Rahal was an IndyCar legend, and he had recently partnered with David Letterman, who was also a major race car enthusiast. They had a new group of cars that would be racing in this event, and David would also be there to do a segment for his late-night show. What made this job very cool for me was Mario Andretti was also at the event, and we spent a good part of the first day shooting fun stuff with him. Mario is a really cool guy, and he was just having fun with us. The production company had purchased a racing helmet, so we shot video of Mario riding around the track in a golf cart wearing the helmet, and other fun stuff. When the two-day shoot was finished, and we had shot all of the scenes with David Letterman, we were packing up and leaving and the production team asked me if I wanted the helmet. I had mentioned to them that a couple years before, I had built a really cool go-cart for my son, Kasen, with a blue fiberglass race car frame. This helmet would be really cool to give him, so of course, I was happy to get this.

As Hugh, my sound guy, and I were walking out to the parking lot, we passed Mario's tent, and I asked Hugh for a Sharpie pen. He did not have one on him, and asked why, so I told him I would love to ask Mario to autograph the helmet for my boy. We just kept walking, and I heard a voice behind me say, "I have a Sharpie!" I turned around to see Mario Andretti walking right behind us, close enough to have heard my wish! He was happy to sign the helmet, and I was thrilled to bring it home to my son, who had no idea who Mario Andretti was. But sometime soon he will know, and what a great memento to give to him. Thanks Mario! You're awesome!

Bark Angels 2014

During my time between COPS seasons, and while Rhino was still an active studio, I was busy between studio time, setting up for client shoots, and making sure all of the gear was properly working and in place. That was really my job while we had the studio. Cliff was busy booking clients, and just being Cliff. But at the end of the day, it was my job, if I was home, to make sure all of the gear was in working order. I needed to make sure the stands were set up, the flags were in place, the monitors were giving a video signal, and the bar was stocked. It was the least I could do, since I was a partner in this amazing studio. The fact that I was also a musician, and Cliff had just found a way to lease the building right next to us and turn it into a recording studio, was just really crazy fantastic to me. The recording studio looked amazing, and was connected to our film studio via a back door. So how can you really go wrong? We had both great spaces ready for any creative means needed.

I had worked with Cliff's friend, Ann Marie, several times in the past with Cliff, and she was running an internet radio station next door. One day she introduced me to Suzie. Suzie was a friend of Ann Marie's, and had a show on the radio called Keeping it Real with Suzie. It was a conversation format about every day circumstances and social platforms. Ann Marie introduced Suzie to me because she had recently been offered a position to host a TV show about service dogs. Since Suzie is a huge animal lover and rights activist for dogs, she was perfect to host this show. She was not very familiar with the person who was offering her the position, and as they had yet to hire a cameraman, Ann Marie felt it would be good for us to chat to see if I could be of any help. Suzie was a strikingly beautiful woman, and she is British, so she has that wonderful British accent. She was really engaging, so I could see why someone would be interested in having her host a show. We talked for a bit, and when she was answering my questions about the show and the person offering her the position, it sounded kind of weird. First off, he told her he was going to buy a network, and that he would have many shows she could be a part of. Seriously? Oprah buys a network. Ted Turner buys a network. Some old guy investing in real estate in Tampa does not buy a network. He was blowing smoke as far as he could just so he could impress her, was my honest opinion.

Suzie felt the same way, so I agreed to meet with her and him at a local restaurant to discuss his offer, and I could help her determine just how full of shit he was. Well, the meeting went great, in the fact that I was able to see this guy was as full of shit as a clogged toilet. When he told me that he was going to buy a network, I laughed and told him that was basically impossible, but good luck. He was a very large man, as in not tall but wide, and he had a younger man with him who I'm assuming was his intern. He was the note taker, and would get us drinks. After a lot of questions and some drinks, he told me he didn't really have a budget for the show, so I told him I would create a budget to shoot the show, and would get back to him with it. You never know for sure if someone is all talk, but we be both still felt that more than likely it was just that. He had told Suzie she would be making so much money, and that her future fame and fortune where all there for the taking! As we left the meeting, Suzie looked at me and said, "Well that sounds like a complete bunch of bullshit!" I couldn't disagree with her, but I had agreed to put a quote together to break down what filming a show like this could cost, if he was serious about doing it right. I worked on a proposal that made sense to me. We would need a sound/editing person, myself as camera and lighting, and

Suzie's day rate as the host. And to save money, I even inserted a rental RV, so we could all travel from place to place together, and our editor would be able to work on the show as we were shooting it at each location. Suzie presented the proposal to her client, and he, of course, responded with, "That's way too much money! We will just have some college interns shoot it for free." This is a normal response from anyone who really does not have any idea what it costs to shoot a show, or the time it takes to put a show together. This guy wanted everyone to work for free, on the prospect that it would be a great show and something he could play on his own network, at little to no cost. Most importantly, it justified our belief that he did not have the massive capital to create a network. He was just completely full of shit.

Suzie and I spoke about it, and we both decided that although his idea was not a horrible one, why would we do all the work for free and have him own the show? It's something we could at least try to shoot and produce ourselves. If it looked like we had something to work with, then we could at least see what we could do with it. What did we have to lose?

With my law enforcement background, and her hosting background and social network of dog trainers, we knew we could get some cool stuff on camera. We first met with a canine trainer who had worked with cadaver and recovery dogs. She also had contacts with other dog trainers, so very quickly we were on a roll. Our first shoot was with a little pup that was in training to become a Diabetes service dog. His daddy was a truck driver, and had recently been diagnosed with this disease. The pup was being trained to alert his owner whenever he detected his scent start to change. The disease was new to this man, and he was not yet able to pick up the early signs when he was about ready to go into an episode. But the dog was able to tell very early on, and would alert the man to check his levels and take insulin if needed. I am not a doctor, so don't quote me on this, but that is my understanding of how it works.

Dogs are incredible animals, and their senses are so much more superior than ours in many ways. This man's career meant he was often on the road, driving a huge truck for hours at a time. So this little pup would be able to travel with him, and be right there to alert him if he picked up the scent that his owner needed to check his insulin levels. It really was very compelling, and the trainer explained how it worked.

They had taken samples of the man's smell during an episode when his insulin levels where off, and his skin would permeate a specific scent, totally different to only the dog's nose. The trainer would then have the man remove his socks after such an episode, and place them in the freezer until she came back for the next training session. During the next session, she would then pull the socks from the freezer, and hide them so the pup would have to find them based on the scent. Suzie and I both thought this was really cool, that you could train a dog to smell a scent from someone going into an insulin dependent state, just based on their sweat glands.

Dogs are truly incredible, and honestly the trainers are just as amazing. This was going to be a great show!

Our next scheduled shoot was with the recovery and cadaver dogs. We were scheduled to meet at a frequent training place they used, which was an old concrete dump facility. It had tons of old concrete slabs and rubble piled up into four-story mountains of debris. It was actually a really cool place, and perfect for what we were about to shoot.

Our shoot would be to hide Suzie in a pile of rubble way down, and let the recovery dog find her. This was similar to when a building would collapse, and the dog could locate her based on scent alone. We both remembered when 9/11 happened, and they brought in K9s to help find the people buried in the rubble. So it was actually quite surreal to see how these amazing dogs are trained to locate possible victims, or survivors, or both after such a tragedy.

Suzie booted up and wore a protective helmet. I gave her a walkie-talkie so we could communicate, and then we basically buried her after she squeezed into a hole formed in the rubble. Then we covered up the entrance with wood pallets and smaller lumps of cement. I have to say, I was a bit concerned that the rubble would collapse, and Suzie would actually get hurt, but she was game, and said, "Let's make it as realistic as we can, but please try not crush me if possible!" I just had to cross my fingers and hope everything would go okay.

Fortunately, it worked out well. I put a wireless mic on her, and grabbed many different angles so I could edit it together. I had to ask them to do a couple of dog maneuvers a couple of times, so I could get different angles for editing. At the end of the day, the search and rescue dog ran across the field and up the hill formed of concrete rubble, and was able to locate Suzie almost immediately. His alert was to sit and start barking when he picked up on the scent of someone hidden under a pile of concrete. It really was incredible to witness, and did make for a nice episode showing just how talented these dogs are.

Next, was the cadaver dog. I had placed a GoPro camera on his harness, and his trainer explained how the training worked. She would place a human rib deep into the woods without the dog being present. When they're ready to start practicing, she instructs the dog to go look, and he runs off tracking a scent until he finds the remains of a smell he is trained to hone in and look for. It was amazing to us both that you could literally train a dog to decipher one scent from another. This dog could smell the difference between a pig bone and a human bone! Animal bones are common in the woods, so you need to train a cadaver dog to be able to detect between the scent of human remains from animal remains. What I thought was cool was that you can actually buy human bones online!

There is a website called the Bone Room, and you can just pick and choose what bones you would like, and they will ship them right to your door! It could be a skull, or femur, or a shoulder blade. Whatever you wish it is available at the Bone Room.

We chased the cadaver dog through the woods, and eventually he detected the smell of this small human rib. When he did, his alert signal was to sit down, a common alert signal, so we knew he had found the remains.

We got great coverage, and mostly everything worked okay. I really hoped to get at least a few decent clips of the search from the dog's perspective on the GoPro, but unfortunately, the camera had flipped upside down once the dog started running. So we got some really cool footage at the beginning, but not all of it. This happens, especially with these tiny little cameras. I would have loved to try it again, but it had already been a long day of shooting, and everyone was ready to call it a day. We still got enough footage to make the show work, as far as putting together a pilot. We shot so many mini episodes, including drug dogs and attack dogs, and had ideas for all sorts of specially trained service dogs.

One of my memories from this time was prepping for the day. When you are a solo crew, it is so hard to think of everything you will need when you are loading gear. I forgot a boom pole the day we were scheduled to meet the K9 Police in a junkyard that they use for training. When it came time for the interviews, I did not have what I needed to make this happen, so I had to create something on the fly.

I found a pole in the junkyard, and taped a mic to it, to get the overhead interviews. It worked fine, that's just a part of the show, and I still learn every time I have to do a solo gig. There are just so many moving pieces and parts, it's not always easy to anticipate or remember to bring everything you may need, but you can usually make it work with a little creative engineering.

After several days of shooting some amazing shows, we had the opportunity to shoot a very special episode. One of the trainers that Suzie had been in contact with had connected Suzie with a trio of fabulous ladies. Suzie was introduced to a lady named Gigi, who had a Giant Poodle named Pete, who was her service seeing eye dog. Gigi's story in and of itself, was very compelling. She had lost her sight in her early twenties, at the hands of her ex-husband. While she was trying to move into a new home in an attempt to escape her increasingly abusive marriage, the husband turned up and literally shot her in the face with a shotgun, point blank.

How she didn't die immediately, only God knows, but she is honestly one of the most amazing people either of us had ever had the honor of meeting. She has the most infectious, upbeat spirit. There is no feeling sorry for herself in the slightest, and we listened to her story of how she had to learn to function again without her sight. She loved her companionship with Pete the poodle, and she totally spoiled him rotten. The poor boy had all sorts of allergies and issues himself, and we were convinced Gigi was his service partner, and not the other way around. We all joked that it seemed Pete could not see either, because, as Gigi would giggle, he would often bump her into walls, etc. We were not sure how compelling Pete's story would be as a service dog, but it didn't matter. Gigi lives with her incredible Mom, Clarice, and together with her sister Rebecca, they had a little trio of amazing humans. All three of them made for such a powerful force of great attitudes, and honestly, a great example of what truly good humans are.

When we first met with these ladies, we not only heard about Gigi's story, but also learned that Rebecca had recently been diagnosed with terminal cancer. Rebecca had been receiving chemotherapy, and was dealing with the hair loss and fatigue as best as she could, and yet still trying to live life to the fullest. She told us about her bucket list of things she wanted to do while she still could.

Rebecca had already been skydiving, and one of the things she said she had yet to accomplish was to race go-karts! When we left the meeting that day, Suzie was determined to help make that happen, and I figured we could film it. If not for the show, then at least for prosperity for the family. We both felt that these ladies alone could have their own show, because they were honestly such incredible characters, and if we could do this with them, it would be an honor to be a part of, regardless of the outcome. We located a racetrack that was willing to let us film Rebecca on her race car day outing with her Mom, Gigi, and of course, Pete the poodle. Suzie had a friend who owned a limo service, and she was able to ask to have the girls picked up in style, and bring them to the racetrack. We arrived at the location early so I could place GoPro cameras on all of the karts, and when the girls arrived we were ready to start shooting. What a great experience! That day truly was for not only us, but for everyone involved. As Suzie said "You don't meet these incredible women, and not feel changed by the experience."

I was able to shoot some amazing footage of them pulling up in the limo, and got them in the race cars after a brief overview from the staff, and then off they went. Rebecca and Suzie went crazy on the track, and were able to race around the track giggling and laughing. The staff even got Gigi and Pete into a golf cart, and drove them around the track, so she could at least feel the wind on her face. A lot of people came together that day to make the experience as special as it possibly could be, and I am forever grateful for it. I was able to edit together so many wonderful shots of Rebecca racing around the track with Suzie, as well as the shots of Gigi and Pete riding around the track. Rebecca had also given me video she had from completing the skydive from her bucket list.

I was so pumped after the success of the day, that I started putting this show together as soon as I got home. I knew it was going to be amazing, and it was. The content was great, and as we watched it later, we could not do so without having tears come to our eyes. We did not know how we could incorporate it into the dog show idea. But we knew, if nothing else, we had great footage to put together, and had something to give the family that would forever document such a beautiful moment and a great day.

This ended up being one of the very last active things Rebecca was able to accomplish from her list. She was an absolute trooper to the very end, and we both visited her in the hospital, along with her Mom and Gigi. As usual, no matter how much inner pain they were all dealing with, they still managed to smile and laugh.

On a personal level, this whole experience came at a time in my life where I truly needed it. My marriage had been falling apart for quite some time, and I really felt lost, confused, and honestly depressed. Just being able to be part of this experience really lifted my spirits when I needed it the most.

Most people I know have to have a job to support their family, purchase a home, buy food, and live a normal life. A normal life to most is a 9-5 job, or some type of schedule that allows them the income they need to survive. It usually offers them time to be at home with their family, if they are married or have children. My career is a real test to find balance and happiness, which is a down side. When I first found this passion, it was very exciting and fun. Not to say that it's not fun anymore, because it most certainly is, but it can take a real toll on any normal relationship. At first, my wife was very positive about me pursuing this career, as it could mean financial stability for the both of us, and it did for some time. But after our son was born, it created a lot of tension, as my travel time became more significant, and my time at home became less and less. This, unfortunately, was leading to our marital demise. It took me about six months to finish editing all the footage for Bark Angels, because I was doing it in between moving out of my family home, still working film jobs, and taking care of the studio. Once I put it all together, honestly, it came out really well. The show looked really nice, and it was a project Suzie and I were both really proud of.

The other amazing thing that happened during this time was the relationship I developed with Suzie. I was going through my marriage breaking up, and she was, as she called it, "officially sworn off ever dating again". We were just two people going through our own challenging experiences in life, and because neither of us were even close to being ready for a relationship, we formed an almost kinship. We enjoyed spending time together, without the pressure of it being anything more than a fun, solid friendship. I would say, and I think Suzie would agree, that shared experiences while filming this show definitely helped us form an awesome friendship, and although we didn't know it then, we would later become more than friends.

One lesson I learned from this experience was that even though I know how to create and shoot and edit a show, I am clueless when it comes to pitching a show. I learned how hard it is to get the show to the right people. Neither of us regret a moment spent putting this show together, because we had a lot of fun making it. We were still in contact about six months after my marriage broke down, and Suzie and I ended up dating. Suzie is still my best friend, but now I also consider her my soul mate. We met trying to get a show about service dogs off the ground, and even though that didn't go anywhere, we have the experience to be thankful for, because we found each other. Now years later, we live together and have three incredible dogs of our own. If we owned more property I believe we would have a livestock of pets!

Emeril's Florida
1-6-2012

Around October of 2012, Bill Mills called me and told me about a new series he was going to be a part of. The show was called Emeril's Florida, and the premise was Emeril Lagasse, a master chef, would visit restaurants all over the state of Florida and watch them cook, display their signature dishes, and talk about how they were inspired to create the dishes.

It was a low budget TV series, and we were working with a shoestring crew, so Bill wanted me to be a part of the crew as a camera assistant, as well as the only grip. The rate was low, but the perk would be we would stay in the finest hotels and eat amazing food every night. Well, how could I say no to that? Plus, it was going to be about two full months of work, so I was happy to say yes. Not just because of the cool experience, but I always loved working with my great friend Bill.

This first season was, to say the least, AMAZING! Holy cow! Emeril was so very gracious to us as a crew. One of our first locations to film was his restaurant in Orlando, called Top Chop. After we finished shooting, he had a special table reserved for all of the crew, and we ate like kings. The food and wine just kept coming, and the flavors were insane.

The season was very much like this most every night, nice hotel rooms, wonderful dinners, and great conversation. The days were tough and long, but the evenings more than made up for the hard work. Emeril is really a down-to-earth, friendly person, who just really knows his skills and is supportive to the people around him.

I personally enjoyed working with him, and I felt we had a solid appreciation for each other. I was busting my ass every day, setting lights and adjusting stands, as well as making sure Bill's camera was set and balanced, and monitors were set up. It was a non-stop day for me every day.

I actually got to the point that when the day was done, I no longer wanted to go out for dinner, because I was just too friggin' tired! However, I was happy just to be a part of this show.

The second season introduced two new crewmembers that I had never worked with in the past, Bill Mumford and Jack Knew. Bill and Jack had spent years working for 48 Hours on CBS, so their background was news magazine formats which was different from what Bill Mills and I were doing. But they brought a new fresh enthusiasm to the table, and we all became life-long friends in a matter of days. Bill Mumford was a good 'ole country boy camera guy, who lives on a ton of land and can light the heck out of an interview, and Jack is really a jack of all trades. Jack and Bill would travel the country in Bill's pickup truck full of gear to whatever location they were told to be at, and then Jack would pull all of this gear out and set it up. Mumford would fine-tune the lights, and create instant awesome interview lighting. So, it did make sense to add them to the Emeril crew for season two, and I immediately felt a friendship with both of them. I love talented, friendly, good people, and I knew I could learn a lot from both of them. So. welcome to the crew, boys! Bill Mills was the Director of Photography for the show and Bill Mumford was the second camera operator/ 2nd unit DP, and they really did work together well. I just took orders from whoever told me to do stuff, so I was always busy.

Jack was a machine and worked non-stop! He was helping me set up lights, and then jumping to his mixer board, and then placing a mic on Emeril and whoever he was interviewing, and working sound. And then after the shot was over, he would help me wrap the gear so we could travel to the next location. We had a great second season, and worked like a well-oiled machine. So when season three came around, we received a bigger budget, and Bill was able to get me a grip crew.

This was awesome, because Bill created a hop-scotch format for setting up the locations. We all met at the first location to light and set up, and then the other grip crew would travel with Bill to the next location and pre-light, so we could save a ton of time and get on with our day. We were knocking out 5 or 6 restaurants a day, and getting great stuff on camera.

So much of what I have learned in this industry, as far as lighting, is what I have learned from Bill Mills. Bill has won multiple Emmys and Cine Golden Eagles for his work, and was nominated for a Primetime Emmy in Cinematography for his work on the National Geographic special "Tigers of the Snow". He understands simple or dramatic lighting, and how to achieve it. Photographers have a natural eye. It's just a gift you were either born with, or you were not. It's like being a painter, you are just born with a creative visual eye.

I have always believed I have had this eye. As a child, I was always drawing and creating pictures on paper. Now, as an adult, I create pictures on film or a digital medium. Sometimes a client wants a quick, simple lighting setup, and Bill can create that for them, or they want a dramatic lighting scheme and that takes more time. I have watched him light amazing scenes in a short amount of time, because for him, it's just easy and makes sense. Working with people like Bill was dramatically improving my lighting skills as well. I really started developing my own understanding of lighting, and was becoming more and more confident in the scenes I was lighting.

Curtis told me once, "If a scene looks lit, then it was lit wrong. If it looks natural, like it was just a normal room, or light coming in from the windows, then it was lit correctly." This sounds simple enough, but since we normally shut off all of the lights in a room and relight from scratch, then this statement should make a whole lot more sense. Imagine walking into your living room at night and shutting off all of the lights. It would pretty much be pitch black, right? Now relight it and make it look natural and real. Have the moonlight or daylight come through the windows and create a shadow on the opposing wall, while the available natural light fills the room, all created by lighting equipment. Yeah, now this sounds a little more difficult to create. Yet you still need to make it look real, like walking into your home every day. These were the tricks of the trade, and I was really starting to get comfortable with this.

We continued Emeril's show for a couple more seasons, but the show came to an end, as most shows eventually do. One very memorable experience on this show was when we were going to shoot the Ice Bar. This was a bar in Orlando that was totally made of ice. It was a really cool concept, as you had to put on a thick coat to go in and have a vodka, sitting at a table on a chair totally made of ice. The entire room is made of ice, and they have cool lighting, and the experience is awesome.

Unfortunately for us, you're not allowed to be in the room for more than ten minutes, because of the extremely low temperature. Not only did we have a lighting set up that would take about twenty minutes minimum, when we got there it was pouring rain outside, so we were all soaked! We had to grab all of the gear outside in the rain, bring it into this Ice Bar, and then grab a coat, and set up for the shoot. We knew with make-up and whatever, it would take another twenty minutes before we could shoot. Bill and I were freezing cold, and we were just looking at each other like, "WTF?" and trying to set up a shot without icicles forming on our "lower regions."

Emeril did finally come in, take a shot, and talk about the bar, which lasted about three minutes. Then we were wrapped, and Bill and I had to take the lights and camera down. Then we drove to our hotel soaking wet and freezing, and saying "We quit!" knowing we were both

just joking. But we still griped about it for the next two days. This did become a common occurrence, but that's why we are
Such great friends.

New Jobs from New Friends

After Emeril's Florida was over, Bill Mumford and Jack Knew both called me to work on other jobs! They liked my work ethic, and appreciated my knowledge for lighting and grip work. Mumford put me on some amazing 48 Hours shoots, as he was a CBS freelancer, and he did a lot of 48 hours shows for them. The first CBS 48 Hours shoot Mumford hired me for was a classic story about Benji Novack, who was the son of Miami royalty Benjamin and Bernice Novack, who owned the famed hotspot Fontainebleau Miami Beach Hotel. This hotel was famous in the 60's, with such guests as Frank Sinatra and John F. Kennedy. When the family lost their fortune and the hotel, Benji was inspired to start his own business planning conferences for corporate clients, and this earned him millions of dollars. Novack had a yacht, a massive Batman memorabilia collection, including a replica of the Batmobile, a wife, and a mistress. Novack was brutally murdered in a hotel room in Miami, and our job was to interview people surrounding the case, so many years later. This is a normal day for the CBS 48 Hours crew, and I was able to be a part of some really interesting murder mysteries! We went to several locations, interviewed a ton of eyewitnesses, and captured some really cool footage. I only worked about three days on this with Jack and Mumford, but I knew I was hooked, and wanted more of these gigs!

The next one Mumford called me on was only about a month later. The reason I became someone to hire was because I was not only a hard worker and understood lighting, but I was also, at the time, a GoPro guru! GoPro is a mini camera that was newly out on the market, and the news agencies were starting to like what they saw with this footage. Jack and Mumford knew I was very familiar with these little cameras, as we had used them on Emeril's Florida, and the CBS producers wanted to use them as well. So, I was the person to get! It is always helpful to have a niche in the industry.

Our next episode was called "Pain and Gain", and what made this so interesting was a feature film had been made about this same story, and was getting ready to be released to the theaters. CBS wanted to get the actual news story out before the feature film was to be released, so it was a race for time! This murder mystery story, again in Miami, was about three meatheads who spent all of their time working out in the gym, and trying to make money. They decided to kidnap a rich guy and force him to transfer all of his assets and money over to them. The situation went insanely wrong, and they killed him, so they had to hide his body. Then they tried to move on to the next target, but it all went sideways, and they were all eventually caught after years of bad ideas and stupid decisions. The entire premise did make for a great movie, but before this would make the theaters, we had to create an actual news story utilizing a lot of the real people involved. My first day on set was in a swamp, and they wanted shots of alligators, since this portrayed the Miami swamplands. They had employed a gator handler to guide us through the swamps and make sure everyone was safe, including the gators. I took a GoPro camera, attached it to the end of one of Mumford's light stands, and placed it into the water right next to the gator's mouth. I honestly had no idea what it would look like, but I just kept pushing the stand left to right, about a foot or so from the gator's mouth, wondering if he would just eat my camera or not. Hey, I knew CBS would buy me a new one if he ate it! Next, the handler wrangled some snakes, and placed them in the water for me to shoot video of, and that also went well. These shots came out great, and later became the opening sequence for the episode!

After we got the gator shots, we moved on to all of the other crazy aspects of this documentary. We shot interviews, and then B-roll of places they had done insane things at. We shot B-roll at restaurants, hotels, and expensive car dealerships. Anything that had some interesting element to the story. Another fun fact was at the time we were shooting this, the TV show Dexter was very popular. So, I decided since I was in Miami, why not Google the Dexter location? I did this and found the address for Dexter's condo! I spent my day off driving to find the location, actually found it, and creeped across a fence line to get a better photograph to send to Suzie and share on Facebook!

I remember we had a studio rented for interviews, and at one time they wanted handcuffs, which I actually had in my car so I pulled those out for the story. This show was so much fun to work on, not only because I was able to listen and learn about a crazy mystery, but I was able to be a part of it! Another interesting part of shooting these types of news programs, is when you are actually in a location where something crazy happened, like a murder or a kidnapping. We shot the actual bathroom in a warehouse where one of the victims had been handcuffed to the sink for a week, and was brutally tortured. Looking at this dark bathroom, you could almost visualize what must have happened. Once the story is finished, and you are heading back home, you have so many more questions! We did a couple more CBS gigs after this, but getting back home and watching them on TV really is the fun moment.

CBS would always send us an email letting us know when a show would air, so we could watch it.

Jack and Mumford put me on several other jobs as well. My point is, if you are willing to work hard and have a great attitude, it's amazing how many other jobs you will get in the future. The bottom line is this, just enjoy the fact that your worst day at work in the industry is so much better than being the ditch digger down the road. It's easy for me to say that, because when I was a kid going to school, I was that ditch digger. I appreciate that I have a camera in my hands today, and not a shovel.

House Hunters

After COPS, I started working back at HSN a little, between Bill and Curtis jobs. One day, I was hired as an AC, or assistant camera, to a friend of mine, Chris Buck. Chris would sometimes work with HSN as a cameraman. Chris and I always got along great, and worked together really well. We were shooting some promo and chatting. I was telling him about some adventures I had on COPS, and he mentioned a show he had been shooting for several years now called House Hunters, and that they were getting so busy he might want to send me on a couple shows. Shooting with a handheld camera requires some special skills, and it's not easy to keep steady after having a 37lb camera on your shoulder for eight hours. I told him I was definitely interested, as I'm always looking for a new adventure.

Chris called me about a month later and had the perfect show to try me out. It was a one-day shoot called "Where Are They Now?" These are homeowners who already have done a show, but then they rehab the property. We come in, and shoot all of the things they have fixed up. Sometimes it's a full renovation, sometimes it's just a couple of rooms. This shoot was up in the Panhandle, so it would be a bit of a drive. Chris explained that the reason he gets all of these jobs is because he agrees to work as a local, meaning there's no travel pay, they only pay for actual shoot days. I think he said he would cover a little of my expenses, like gas and tolls, but that was all he could pay.

I gave it some thought because that's a lot of travel time from where I lived. Fourteen hours of travel there and back for a one-day job, but I was available, so what the heck? My producer's name was Susan Hull, and the homeowners were a gay couple who had totally redone their condo. The shoot was a blast! The homeowners were way fun, and Susan is a fabulous producer, and we hit it off just great. Apparently, I got a good review from Susan, because the next thing I know, Chris is lining me up with work! The show is a blast to shoot, and the days are very fair.

House Hunters has been an amazing chapter in my career, and similar to other shows I have done, I have put together a kind of journal of some of my more memorable shoots. I hope you enjoy reading about them as much as I enjoyed reminiscing about them.

Birmingham, AL 10-19-13

This was the first job Chris sent me on with Tom Hurxthal. Tom is a sound guy, and he is a little older than me, and very friendly. He lives in Sarasota, and I lived in Parrish at the time, which meant we were only about 30 minutes apart. So it made sense to put us together as a team, so we could ride together to the airport, and only pay for one car in long term parking.

Tom and I had worked together once before, a year earlier at a baseball function, and I remembered him being a pleasure to work with.

We were scheduled to fly to Birmingham, Alabama to do a shoot with Robert Holberg. Robert has been producing House Hunters for many years, and this shoot was for a young couple that were buying a larger house. Stacy and Matt were young professionals, who both had really well-paying jobs, so they had a larger budget and were also upsizing, as they were getting ready to start a family. They were both very nice people, with fun attitudes, and they were both super excited to be on the show. Some of our shots were following them out to the golf course, and showing them swinging long shots down the fairway. One of their priorities for the new home was to have a room that they could put their foosball table. They loved to play foosball, as they had met at a party playing foosball.

The production company that shoots and puts together House Hunters is called Pie Town. Pie Town has a staff of producers in Los Angeles, and part of their job is to go online to find, call, and schedule places for us to shoot B-Roll with the homeowners. Since one of their requirements was to have a room for their foosball table, someone at Pie Town Googled "bar with foosball tables", and found a little hole in the wall called The Upsidedown Plaza. Robert, Tom and I all showed up before the homeowners to scope out the location, so I could determine lighting needs. We were in downtown Birmingham, and the bar was underground, so the three of us walked down the subway style stairs to open the bar door. What we found inside looked like a small corner of Hell! Well, Hell with a lot of neon lighting. The bar was very dark, of course, but one of the more interesting elements to this wonderful little watering hole, was the massive amount of sexual graffiti all over the walls. Seriously, I'm not exaggerating when I say this. From floor to ceiling, it seemed every patron that had ever come in had taken some type of colorful ink marker, and wrote some very prolific statements. Phrases like "Suck my big fat *%#@!", or

"Eat this" (with a very unappetizing drawing to explain what needed to be eaten) absolutely covered the walls.

Yes, there were advertising signs all over as well, but fortunately for us, we did not have to cover many logos. Most of them had already been covered by enlarged pictures of penises or breasts.

To add to the fun factor of this charming little venue, there was the human element. I am sure you can imagine the quality patrons who were spending their Thursday morning enjoying a frothy mug of brew. I would have to guess the only three people in the building who did not have an outstanding warrant were our crew. Robert was beside himself, as this was not exactly what he had imagined, so I went up to the bar to talk to the bartender about us shooting there. He was aware that we were supposed to film there, but I don't think he actually gave two shits. Apparently, the owner's wife loves the show, so they were told to let us in and do whatever we needed to do.

This was really a great icebreaker for me to be able to work with Robert for the first time, because it was hard to stop laughing. Everywhere we turned, there was more graffiti, or a less than desirable image on a wall. The foosball table was in the corner next to the bathroom, and that was also just as educational. I think I learned a couple new words while relieving myself of my morning coffee.

So, we set up some small lights, and decided to just try to frame out as much as we could. We used tight shots, and tried to rack out the background focus as best we could. I was just hoping we could do this quickly, before any of the locals decided to make one of us their next cellmate!

We walked back upstairs outside to be greeted by our two homeowners…wearing Argyle sweaters and boat shoes, looking like they just came from a Polo match. My first thought was that they are never going to live through this, Matt will be shanked before we even start rolling. I took one look at him, and busted out laughing. I tried to explain to Robert that we might want to consider a wardrobe change, and I think he understood, but it was hard to tell over his laughter. Tears were literally rolling down our faces.

These little gifts of fun are the moments we still talk about. We got through the shoot, and the homeowners did fine, even though I know they were very uncomfortable in the environment. But, hey... you can't really put a price on this kind of entertainment.

Pittsburg, PA 11-26-14

This was an interesting story. Allison and Alysa. A 50 year old, recently divorced, mom of three tours homes with her oldest daughter, Ally, to try to find a new home for her and her two sons and dog. Ally, who was in town from college, tours the homes with her, as we always have a two-person talent group for the show. She was looking for a three-bedroom home with a nice kitchen, because she loves to cook. She was also looking for a home that has a large backyard, because she plays with her dog every morning at 5am while having her coffee.

They toured three homes with us, but as usual, we had to split up the show so we could come back and show the purchase home, once she had moved in. We are always hoping that one of the homes we tour becomes the home they purchase, and if not, we have to wait. Anything can happen, a loan could fall through or there could be a bad inspection. You just never know with real estate deals.

The issue with this episode in particular, was that we were on the brink of winter. So even though the skies were clear when we started, there was concern that with the weather starting to get cold, and a nor'easter coming in, when we came back in two or three weeks we may have snow, which would look strange.

Pittsburgh is a beautiful city with very friendly people, and drivers who stop to let you pass, and wave at you to drive in front of them. The houses are very Northern looking and simple, usually two stories, with basements and a lot of character. I have always loved brick-based homes, as they remind me of the house I grew up in up north. Allison found her home with a nice kitchen, although she planned to completely renovate it, and she liked the rest of the house. The house was front lit by the sun, so we were able to shoot the house well, as the sun would shine through the windows and light the house nicely. We did have to light a couple of rooms, but they all looked nice. While framing the outside, I was careful not to show much of the side yard, as I knew when we came back there would probably be snow on the ground, and that is exactly what had happened. Three weeks later when we came back in town, there was about six inches of snow on the ground! We shot around this as best as we could, and the show came out fine, but if you look closely you can see some shots have green grass and some have snow. Most people are not paying attention to that too much, as long as the story you are telling is compelling. This would become more and more common, I would learn, as the winter seasons would come and go.

Wilson, NC 12-6-14

The homebuyer's names were Brent and Liz. Wilson is a very small town about forty-five minutes south of Raleigh, North Carolina. The home costs are low, and the real-estate market is not booming, so you can get a lot of home for your money. This day would have been fairly routine, but every once in a while, you get a bunch of production roadblocks in your way. Those roadblocks started when we were backing into the driveway. Tom looked across the street, and said, "Oh, goodie, a man with a chainsaw." Lawn equipment is a soundman's worst nightmare, as the microphones we use are extremely sensitive, and pick up every ambient sound. It's not good when you hear a sound, but cannot see what is making the sound. So chainsaws, leaf blowers, and lawn mowers are all a bad sign for a production crew. Then, we started hearing drums, followed by trombones, far off in the background.

It turned out that morning the Wilson Holiday Parade was running, and to add to that, the weather was going to turn bad in about an hour. The sky was overcast, so we decided to try to shoot all of our outside stuff right away, before the band played and the rain came. Some days you got lucky and some days you didn't. That was one of our lucky days, as we managed to get walk up dialogue scenes between the trombones and chainsaws, and our backyard scenes as well.

One funny note I remembered was as soon as we started shooting, I had framed up my shot tight on Brent getting out of the driver's seat, and as soon as we rolled camera, a car pulls right into the background. We had to cut as we watched this woman, oblivious to us standing across the street, as she slowly took her time getting her groceries and packages out of her car and walked away. It was too funny not to laugh out loud.

After we shot the walk up, we went inside to start shooting, and then heard the rock hammer start next door. They were starting to build that home, and had to smash all of the rocks so they could start the foundation. Oh, goody, just more outside noise. Fortunately, the noise was not horrible inside the house once we closed the doors, so we were eventually able to complete our day. The part of my career that keeps me young, is that you never really have any control of the outside elements in reality TV. You just have to learn how to roll with the punches, and get creative sometimes.

High-Profile House Hunters

In mid-July 2014, Tommy and I were on a shoot in Florida with a couple, and we had a new producer, whose name was Darby Dickerson. She was not new to the company at all, but we had never shot with her. We had a really great shoot, and everyone got along really well. It was one of those shoots that I felt able to get really creative with my shots. Apparently, Darby recognized my ability and willingness to try to get those creative shots. Darby had been working with Pie Town and House Hunters for quite some time, and she really liked the way I shot the show. So when we finished this particular episode, she took me aside and told me she had been requested to shoot a high-profile House Hunters, and asked if I would be willing to travel with her and shoot this show.

Of course, I said yes. She told me the network wanted a very seasoned crew on this shoot, because the home buyers were high-profile television stars, so we all had to be on our best behavior and very professional. I had worked with so many high-profile actors by this point, that I had no problem working with whomever they put us with. We would have a great shoot and have fun, because after a while you just get used to working with a crew, no matter who they are. I had worked with John Travolta, Morgan Freeman, Jonathan Demme, Roy Schieder, Thomas Jane, and Philp-Michael Thomas, to name a few. So, I was happy to work with seasoned professionals again, as it usually makes the entire shooting experience much easier.

This show would be no exception, as the homebuyers were Eric Christian Olsen and his wife, Sarah Wright. They were house hunting in Wyoming, because they love the area and wanted a special vacation home to go to when they were not shooting shows. Eric is well known as Detective Marty Deeks on the CBS series NCIS: Los Angeles, and Sarah has been in several films including Marry Me and American Made. Their busy lifestyle offered them little time to relax, but when they had the time, they wanted a real getaway to destress and chill, and just enjoy God's beautiful scenery.

Our venue was to be Jackson, Wyoming, and we had several homes to shoot and look at during our seven-day trek. We first landed and drove to what was to be our home base in Huntsman Springs, which is just outside of Driggs, Idaho. Huntsman Springs is located in the Teton Valley, and is an amazing community of beautiful homes surrounded by a five-star golf course, as well as the view of the Teton Mountains. Tommy and I had one home, and Darby and her co-producer had another. We had this location offered to us because it was also where one of the homes they were considering was located, so the real estate agency offered for us to stay there. It actually made sense, since we had so much gear we had to work with. I took the main floor bedroom, because it had a Jacuzzi tub. Really, is there anything better than soaking in a Jacuzzi with a glass of wine at the end of a tough day, before you walk out your back porch and watch the sunset? Yeah, I could get used to that.

This was not our normal shoot, but I felt so blessed to be on it! We had a big schedule ahead of us, so Tommy and I unpacked, got the batteries on charge, and checked the gear, before we settled down from the flight.

Our first morning was to meet with Eric and Sarah, and then find an area where we could have them sit down, and shoot the intro interview. This interview allows them to explain why they are looking for a home, and the things they really want, as well as the things they do not want. We found a comfortable spot on a couch with a nice stone fireplace in the background, and started the interview. For me, this was really stressful because the people in front of the camera were industry professionals, and I had to make sure I was really on my game. My color balance, focus, and lighting had to be perfect, as anything I shot will be critically reviewed back in post after the shoot. If I screwed anything up, I could be in trouble.

As far as the camera crew, it was just me. I had to light it and shoot it myself, so I really had to make sure there were no mistakes. We shot a great interview with Eric and Sarah, and Darby asked great questions, and I could tell we were all starting to meld well with each other. This is so important regardless of the talent, but especially important when your homebuyers are television stars.

One thing I noticed during the interview was a misunderstanding of terminology. As Eric and Sarah were speaking and telling a story, Darby would tell them to "make it smaller," and then re-ask the question. They would again, tell the story of their needs and wants, and then Darby would say, "That was great. Now make it smaller." At first, I did not understand the confusion, but as the interview continued, I started to see what was going on. What Darby meant by "make it smaller" was to consolidate your statement. Make it shorter, so we can use it in a thirty second intro. Eric thought it meant lower your enthusiasm, or slow your emphasis in your statement.

This became a bit of a wall between us, because Eric was like "I can't make it any smaller, and why would I?" Darby did not understand what he was trying to say, and as the camera guy, I can't get in the middle of this. It's no one's fault, it's just different terminology between the two different film environments, reality TV vs scripted TV.

We finished the interview, and after we were all done and packing up, Darby and I were talking about the interview, and ways we could make it work better and what went wrong. While we were talking, Eric came back into the room and joined our conversation, and we had a chat about the confusion of terminology. Bottom line, how can we communicate better?

We are all professionals, we just express things a bit differently, that's all. After that, everything went like clockwork. We shot several different locations, and had a blast. Sarah loved a lot of the homes, but in the end, they decided on the Huntsman Springs home because of all the amenities, as well as the view. Most importantly, the builder/designer donates all the profits to cancer research, which in itself is amazing. Please look this place up online, as it is an amazing community, and knowing that the builder donates all profits to cancer research is incredible.

During the tours, two things really stood out for me. First they had their little boy, who they called Bear, with them. He was about four years old, and just adorable. It is hard to be away from your child, which I was, so to see this beautiful boy running around and playing, makes any father think of their child and wish they were home. But when you have to travel to pay the bills, it's what you do. The second thing was Eric, as I really liked him as a person, and by the end of the shoot, I truly considered him a friend. We just seemed to click and understand each other. I still send him pictures of the crazy Clark Griswold inventions I make for my son, and he always has cool responses. He understands being a good father is way more important than any of this other crazy stuff we do. I hope Eric, Sarah and little Bear get to spend a lot of time at this beautiful home they now have, and enjoy the beautiful sunset views of the Teton Mountains. This is truly God's country.

Paducah, KY 12-12-14

The homebuyer's names were Josh and Clint. When I first got the call to shoot House Hunters in Paducah, Kentucky, my first thought was "Where the hell is Paducah?" The name itself screams of a backwoods, redneck, moonshine making town for sure! We drove about two and a half hours from Nashville into Paducah. We found our Best Western hotel, which was truly out in the middle of nowhere, and decided to keep driving into town. Our GPS said a Walmart was two miles away, and that's where we would normally stock up on food and other things to get us through the week. The first thing we noticed as we drove over a small bridge, was the town opened up before us, and had everything. A huge mall, restaurants, fast food, clothing stores, and specialty shops were abundant. The town was thriving! We continued on into the downtown area and wow! Downtown Paducah was so beautiful. The buildings were all historically old, but completely renovated and updated. All of the Christmas lights were up on the buildings, and you could tell this little town was just amazing. Paducah sits at the west end of Kentucky, right at the tip. It rests on the Ohio River, so Paducah has easy access to rail, water, and road transportation. It is very well known for its cultural heritage in the arts and theater. Our couple for this episode was a gay couple who had been married for six years, and were now ready to purchase their first home together. Super fun couple, and great on camera. Darby was producing this episode, and we had a really fun time on this show. We laughed and joked a lot, which really helps make the shoot more fun. The food there is amazing everywhere you go. I really have warm memories of Paducah, and if I could retire anywhere, I probably would put Paducah in the top three places to live out my days. Josh and Clint found a beautiful home they are going to renovate, so they might do a "Where Are They Now?" episode in the future. It would be great to go back!

Tiny House Hunters

This was a special series House Hunters was doing called Tiny House Hunters. It was a show about people who were trying to really downsize their environment, and live in very small homes. The premise was to move into a very, very small home to minimize the family's financial expenses and environmental footprint. Most of these homes were wood based structures, usually built on top of garden trailers. At the time, this was a trending topic for the general public in regards to downsizing, so why not make a show about people who were actually willing to significantly downsize, to the point of living in a built-up garden trailer! The concept of "prepping" was also a big thing on TV, as many shows were about survival and being off the grid. So it made sense to have a show about downsizing and living off the land, so to speak.

Our first show was in North Carolina, and our producer was a guy named Kevin, who had been shooting House Hunters for probably ten years or more. Tiny House Hunters was a new show, so we were all a little confused about how we would fill a full day shooting a garden trailer. Honestly, Tom and I were a little excited, thinking we would have short days, and get back to the hotel at a decent hour every day.

This family was a female firefighter who had recently sent her daughter off to college, and wanted to go from her current 1800 square foot home, to a very small and portable 90 square foot home. These homes are usually on wheels, and can be moved easily with a small pick-up truck, so her idea was to be able to settle down anywhere. If she felt the need to be able to relocate her home somewhere else on a whim, she could easily just hitch it up and go. The trick with this show was, how do you tour a home that is so small? You would think you could shoot this tour in 5 minutes, but the truth was we shot ALL day! You still have to fill the time needed for a thirty-minute show.

The first day was a full day of shooting, as we had the old home, interviews, room shots, and local surroundings to shoot. The next day was a bunch of exterior shots of the tiny home, every corner and element of the exterior, as well as all of the interior shots. Kitchen, upstairs loft bedroom, bathroom, living room, etc. Since the home is so small, we had to spend a lot of time shooting all of the little spaces and compartments that allow someone to actually live and store all of their things. After we would get all of these shots, then we would shoot the tour and ending interview, and then another tiny house the next day. Just like on House Hunters, we would shoot at least three different tiny houses for them to choose from.

This was a cool new show to work on, as you would normally never think about how someone can utilize every little space for storage or for conventional use. Every day was a full day, and what made the tours more interesting was that I am a 6'3", 230lb man in a 90 square foot trailer! To put this in perspective, it would be like shooting in an average size master bathroom. Tom had to stay outside and feed his audio cable through a window, and I would suck in my fat and hide in a corner to shoot the family walking in their new small home, looking at every little thing. Amenities like a mini sink, a mini refrigerator, a mini shower, and a mini kitchen table. All of these things were crazy to light and film, and then have to work around other people in such a small space!

What made this episode even more fun was the homebuyer's boyfriend was my size! Filming him trying to climb up the ladder of this tiny loft was truly hysterical. Even better was when I had to climb up into the loft, and film both of them up there as well!

This show did so well on TV, that they hired a full-time producer, Jeff Uncapher, who we worked with many times over the course of the next year. Jeff was amazing, and he had worked on several shows in the past that were similar to Tiny House Hunters, in regards to them being FYI type of shows.

Jeff had a clear understanding of getting the homeowner to open up and be real. This entire show was based around a new beginning utilizing a small new environment, but also incorporating landscape and simplicity. Jeff was so much fun to work with, and Tom and I probably shot around 30 episodes of Tiny House Hunters with Jeff. Not only did we shoot some great shows as a team, but we became awesome friends. Jeff was also promoted to work on the regular House Hunters format, so Tom and I shot several of those shows with Jeff.

One of our favorite shows was with a retired Air Force pilot who flew Air Force Two for the President and Vice President. He flew dignitaries and the Vice President all around the world as a career. Now that he was retired, his family was looking to settle down and buy a home with some land, so he could grow crops and just enjoy his family and the land.

We started the week at his parents' property, riding on four-wheelers filming around the property, and shooting the kids fishing and taking care of horses in the barn. For me, this was such an enjoyable shoot as when I retire, this would be my dream. So what fun to shoot good people actually living that same dream, just a little older and financially ready for retirement. Honestly, I was a little envious, and I hope to get there someday myself.

What made this shoot even more fun was the friendship we developed during the course of the show. When we first started, the husband was really not excited about being a part of the show. This was so normal! Usually, it is the wife who watches House Hunters, and submits their application. When they actually get accepted for a show, you now have a very excited wife and a less than pleased husband, who has to be a part of the craziness. It is difficult to get the husband excited, and sometimes it can be so difficult that you have to shoot around the husband just so you have enough footage to make the show work! In this case, he came around and really started enjoying our week, and that was because of Jeff! Jeff was really able to get him to lighten up, and be excited about what we were shooting. By the end of the week, we were all such great friends! We actually spent the last day with him shooting city landscape stuff, and had an amazing day! We all had a tear in our eye leaving that shoot.

It is kind of strange, you start a job, commit to that job, and every now and then you attach emotions to what you are shooting, and then abruptly have to leave it. The friendships you develop over a job are unfortunately quick paced and most of the time not long lasting. However, sometimes they do last, and those are the best memories of your career. I have been blessed with this show in particular, to have made so many great acquaintances with newfound friends. Similar to when I was on COPS, but without the bullets and foot pursuits!

Jeff, Tom and I shot so many more Tiny House Hunters episodes, however a series like this will not last forever, and it finally had to end. Jeff is now working for another Los Angeles production company, and he will continue to do amazing work, as that is the most important thing I realized with Jeff. What made him a great producer is he was just naturally a great person, and the talent picks up on that. Not only does it make the day go fast and fun, but the content you get can be amazing!

Baltimore, Maryland 5-30-15

One of the House Hunters I will always remember was in Baltimore, Maryland. A young man named Freddy Grey was apprehended by the police, and subsequently died during apprehension. The town went into a riot because of racial tension. They destroyed and burned several police cars in downtown Baltimore, and burned down several structures, including a CVS building. On May 26th, the mayor instituted a state of emergency and out of state law enforcement and the National Guard were called in. At the same time, we had a new House Hunters family scheduled for filming. The hotel we were staying at was filled to the brim with law enforcement. Around 150 officers were stationed at our hotel.

This was amazing to watch, as after we would wrap and get to the hotel, it was also about the time they were being dispatched to go to work to secure a safe environment for the protesters. During a state of emergency, often a city will call in outside resources to amplify the manpower needed to secure the environment. This was a much-needed resource, as well as very impressive to witness. It also, however, is a bit tough to maneuver through the hallways with gear to get to your room, and a hot shower is not possible, although certainly worth the inconvenience for the safety of the city. Our hotel was filled with the New Jersey Police Department, and the parking lot was full of marked cruisers, unmarked black Tahoes, communications trucks, armed personnel vehicles, as well as two large transport busses to load up the officers for deployment. One of the nights I was outside in the back of the hotel having a smoke was when the entire department came out and lined up in the parking lot in full formation, similar to a military parade.

They were getting ready to deploy, and were going to discuss their tactical plan for the evening. As a photojournalist, I wanted to capture this amazing event, and held out my cell phone to shoot video of it. Immediately, an officer saw me and yelled at me to stop filming. He then came up to me and explained very professionally that they were there to provide a protective service, and that some people would want to harm them for providing that service, and said not to film this event. After all my years working with law enforcement, and having the massive respect for them that I have, I showed them the roughly ten seconds of film I had shot on my phone, and also deleted it right in front of him.

Then he asked if I would leave, so as to not witness the tactical plan they were getting ready to discuss. I totally understood why they did this. I know that, as a journalist, we have a right to shoot anything on public roads or places, including parking lots. But the truth is, if you cause an issue, law enforcement can find ways of detaining you for other reasons, and I did not want to end up in jail when I need to be shooting the next day. More importantly, I just respect law enforcement, and what they are doing, way too much to become one of those asshole photojournalists who just wants to get the shot!

The show went on without a hitch for the most part, other than driving down streets to get to locations that were wall-to-wall with National Guardsmen, tanks, and military vehicles of all kinds. What makes venues like this so interesting is you just never know what situation may occur when you get into a town, and this one made history. So, with respect, we would try to take back roads, and when we were in the hotel, we would try to give them as much space as they needed. It was a bit tricky getting a hot cup of coffee in the morning with 200 Guardsmen in the breakfast line.

The Freddy Grey incident would occupy the news for months after this, and I would continue to watch the feeds long after I was back home. When you remember being in a town that has a history attached to it, good or bad, you reflect sometimes.

I also remember when we were shooting in Aurora, Colorado, and our hotel was literally right next to the Century 16 movie theater, where an insane man went in and shot up an entire theater full of innocent people. He was dressed in full battle gear, and he had dyed his hair orange like the Joker. During the midnight premiere of The Dark Knight Rises, James Holmes entered the theater through the back door thirty minutes into the film, and fired on the crowd. He through smoke grenades into the theater and then started randomly shooting people. Ten victims died at the scene, and two more at the hospital, including a six year-old girl. Seventy people were injured, most from gunfire. Holmes left the theater, but was captured a couple of blocks away. He was sentence to life in prison, without any chance of parole. When Tom and I checked into the hotel, and I looked out my window, it was just very surreal to see the exact movie theater I had seen so many times on TV before! This was just another history making event, and it can be somewhat macabre when you are standing in front of a location that at one time had so much tragedy attached to it.

Nashville, TN 5-22-15

Sometimes you just have to ride the wave when it comes to shooting reality TV. Sound can always be a problem as lawn crews, highway traffic, and construction all create elements of a difficult location. Sometimes it's just the environment, maybe horrible weather or a bad location. Well, this shoot had all of these lovely elements!

Our first tour house, which would wind up being be the purchase house, just happened to be located right next to a vacant lot where big frontend loaders were digging holes into the ground, and guys with jack hammers were breaking up the rocks. It makes it really difficult to try to record testimonials with a construction zone going on in the background.

We did the best we could with the situation, but sometimes you just have to make the call to relocate. The very next day, we showed up to a tour house that just was not going to work for the show. It was completely wrong for what the homebuyers were wanting, but it also had way too much artwork on the walls. Artwork can be a big problem for the show, as we cannot get a release on artwork, so we cannot show it in the background. So when we show up on a house that looks more like an art museum than a living room, we have to decide what to do. Sometimes we will remove the artwork, but if it is just too many pictures, we will try to find another house to tour.

So, the realtor made some calls to find us a different house. She did find one, so the crew packed up and drove a few blocks to this new home, only to find it was still under construction, with no power and stud walls. So we went to a third house. Nice family, and we managed to get our shots. Another house was absolutely jam-packed with Christmas ornaments! Santas everywhere, reindeers in the front yard, and a tree in every room. This is another issue we have to contend with for the show, we are not allowed to date the show. Meaning, they would like to be able to air the show at any month they wish, so it would not make sense to shoot a house full of Halloween decorations for a show that is scheduled to air in mid-July.

Problems like this are pretty common, and part of being in the field is just working around these issues. Sometimes you can spend more time looking for a place to shoot, than actually shooting the show. Other times, really most of the time, you get lucky, and the shoot days go like clockwork.

Columbia, SC 6-27-15

I drove up to this location because it was only eight hours away from home, and that makes it so much easier than flying, renting a car, and lugging all of that gear! I showed up to check in, only to find out that there had been a bad thunderstorm, and that none of the hotel rooms had power. They had been out of power for hours, and no idea when it would be turned back on, as the outage consisted of the entire city block. Luckily for me, since I drove a rental car to this location, I had loaded some extra gear, including a panel light that works off of camera batteries. While everyone else in the hotel had pitch black rooms, everybody hanging outside and smoking cigarettes, I was able to set up a panel light with a battery and light up my room. I pulled a light stand out of the car, placed the panel light on it, and just aimed it at the ceiling, which really illuminated the room quite nicely.

I could see very well in my room and was able to set up my laptop and iPad, as well as hang my clothes and unpack my suitcase. My iPad had its own cellular service, so I was able to find my first location and MapQuest the distance, with basically all the comforts of a hotel room, except for air conditioning. I also used the Wi-Fi on my cell phone to allow my laptop to connect to the internet. Since my laptop had a full battery, I was able to watch TV and movies. You could see all of the other hotel patrons walking past my room in confusion. I kept the door open because it was hot as heck inside my room, but it looked to everyone else like I had the only room with power. Sometimes we could work out our simple issues, like power or AC, because we are prepared with the simple basics. Lesson learned, if you check into a hotel with no power, plug in a battery-operated panel light, and you are just fine while everyone around you is in the dark. Unfortunately, air conditioning is an amenity I have yet learned how to travel with, but with modern day technology, I don't think it will be far away.

Columbus, Ohio 7-10-15

This was a fun show for me, not just because the homeowners were great, but even better was the Christmas Story House! On most shows, we have a day of what we call scenics. This is a day we spend at the end of the show shooting all of the iconic things in a town, like signs, water towers, and significant buildings or bridges, etc. This time, as we looked at the shot list provided by the show producer, one of the places to shoot was the Christmas Story House. Now, anyone who knows me would tell you, I am a Christmas fanatic. I love Christmas, and I love the film A Christmas Story. I grew up watching this movie every year, usually several times each year. I have always had a warm happy feeling about the "House on Cleveland Street", it seemed so kind and simple. Because the story takes place in the 1930s, they did not have a TV, just a radio to listen to Little Orphan Annie. As Mom was in the kitchen making corn beef cabbage on the stove, you know the house smelled amazing. The kids would play out in the snow, and Dad would come home and rustle with the radiator in the basement. God, I love this movie. Anyways, even though the film takes place in Indiana, the actual house they filmed at is in Columbus. So after we finished our day of shooting, Tom and I had two options of places to go check out, The Rock and Roll Hall of Fame, or the Christmas Story House. We both agreed, and we went back and did the full tour of the house and museum. Suzie even got online and bought me the full-size Leg Lamp as a surprise! I had called her to tell her how cool the house was, and that they had a full-size Leg Lamp! She told me to get it for my birthday, which was coming up, but I declined, saying there would be no way I could ever get it on the plane. After I got back to the hotel, she called and said "Surprise! I ordered the lamp and it will be here before you get home." It's just another reason why I love her. She was just being sweet, but I'm sure deep down she regrets that purchase every Christmas, when she watches me set that huge Leg Lamp in the front window of our beautiful home and say "It's a major award!"

This is what makes my job so enjoyable, being able to discover so many fun things all over the United States when you travel. Most of the time you don't even know what you will find until you land.

Santa Claus, Indiana 7-18-15

Santa Claus, Indiana. Wow! What can I say? Yes, it's exactly what you think. Holiday Town, located in Santa Claus, Indiana, is an entire town dedicated to Christmas. Given the fact that I enjoy the Christmas season so much, I was very excited to see this little town. All of the streets have Christmas themed names, like Rudolph Drive, Jingle Bell Way, and Prancer Court. Too much fun! I grew up in Indianapolis, and had no idea this town even existed. We had a great couple to shoot for this episode. The houses shot nicely, and we did some fun activities on a pontoon boat using our GoPro cameras, and even rigged one to roller coaster at the Christmas based theme park. Every once in a while, we are offered the opportunity to do really cool things when it comes to shooting, just because of the fact that we are attached to this really cool show. In this case, I noticed a Condor, which is a lift machine with a basket that will raise you high up into the sky. I asked the management of Holiday Town if they would be willing to let me go up in the Condor, so I could get a really cool shot of the roller coaster coming in from the track. They agreed, so I climbed into the basket, went up about thirty feet, and got an amazing shot of the couple coming in from the ride. If you are a Christmas fan like me, and you are looking for a fun holiday adventure, I highly recommend this as one of your destinations. Just like any theme park type of environment, there will always be some part that just does not seem to quite work, or issues that occur while you are there. This park had many Santas, so we were trying to schedule an interview with one through management. At first, the Santa who was working was not able to meet with us, because he was busy with families, so we shot other parts of the park. This park has so much Christmas stuff to shoot, that the options were endless. There was a candy cane alley, Christmas elves toy making store, and a sleigh builders center. While we were getting ready to pack up, a lady came running out, and said Santa would like to speak with us. A short Santa Claus came sauntering out, and basically told our producer he would only do the interview if "we had a little something for Santa." Then, as he leaned in closer, he informed us that Santa had a rent bill too! What was even more disturbing, was as he invaded our space to tell us he wanted cash, we could tell that he reeked of alcohol! OMG! Santa had been sipping a little too much eggnog! This totally reminded me of when cousin Eddy dressed up like Santa, before kidnapping Clark Griswold's boss in Christmas Vacation! It was really kind of creepy to see a drunk Santa! I also noticed Santa really needed to drop his outfit off to the dry cleaner elves, as his dim red suit was almost as disheveled as he was! I wasn't sure whether to laugh, or to have the crew hide behind me. Obviously, we declined the interview. Fortunately, the next day management had an amazing Santa that did a great interview, and we shot some wonderful segments with him. Thank goodness for a sober Santa Claus! As a side note, just like any theme park based company, not everyone you hire will be an amazing representative of your company. I'm sure this Santa did not last long, as management for Holiday Town was extremely professional, and wanted to make sure that, even with House Hunters, they were represented as such. I'm sure even Disney gets a Goofy instead of a Mickey from time to time.

Traveling with Gear

When traveling with gear, The Boy Scout motto applies: Always be prepared.

When I would shoot for House Hunters, usually I traveled with a sound person. We try to fly on airlines that have very lenient baggage policies or Media Rates, so we can travel with our gear, and not break the bank in luggage and overweight fees. Southwest is a great airline for this at the moment, as they allow media to travel with two cases up to a hundred pounds. What we normally do is travel to the airport early, and one of us will stay with the car at curbside check in, while the other will roll the cases to the check-in and get us all settled. This usually works pretty well, but sometimes things change, and it can become a bit of a mess.

One trip in particular comes to mind. Tom and I were scheduled to do several legs back to back. First in Baltimore for a couple of days, then straight to Columbus for three days, then to Indiana. I had forgotten my media badge, which I had printed on Photoshop and laminated at home, but I was not worried, because Tom usually checks in the gear, and I would stay with the rental car. At one point during our trip, Chris texted us with a change of plans. He wanted Tom to fly out to Alabama to finish a show with another DP, and I would be traveling to Athens, Georgia to finish up a last-minute show, then we would reconnect in Indiana.

This type of change happens from time to time, and you just have to roll with the punches, but the punches can get a bit hard for sure. This meant that I would be traveling alone with all of the gear. Two large cases, full of production gear and lights, a very large tripod case, my personal suitcase, backpack, and the camera. We both flew out of Columbus, just on different planes, so check-in was still fairly easy. Unfortunately, the agent now wanted to see my media badge, which, of course, I had left at home.

After a bit of smooth talking with the lead agent, I was able to get the media rate for the gear.

It's helpful that so many people love House Hunters, and it's amazing what you can get done just by mentioning that you are part of this show. I flew into Atlanta, and was going to drive to Athens from there. Now, for those of you who have never had the pleasure of frequenting the Hartford Regional Airport in Atlanta, IT BLOWS! I got off the plane and went to the baggage claim. Only my suitcase showed up, so after every other bag on the plane had been retrieved, I went over to the baggage claim office, where they informed me that all large cases are placed at the end of the building. That info would have been helpful forty-five minutes earlier. Then, I had to rent a luggage cart and load up all of this gear, a Pelican 1650 case, a Diva DP light case, Tripod case (sideways), suitcase and camera. Pushing the cart twenty feet was not easy, let alone to the other side of the complex. The rental car building is, of course, off site from the airport, so you have to take a train to get there.

Now to get to the train, you have to go across the street, and then up an elevator. The tripod case won't fit through the door sideways, so the cart has to be unloaded to get in the elevator, then reloaded getting out of the elevator. Then you go across a very long covered walkway to another elevator (same deal), then down to the first floor to walk a hundred yards, then yet another elevator to go up to the third floor of the garage to get to the train. Once the train gets to the rental car building, then it's more of the same. After several trips of this, I started to get used to the insanity of the design, but the first time was quite a treat! The one lesson I have learned whenever I have to fly in or out of Atlanta, is give yourself way more time than you think you need, and Xanax, or you will miss your flight.

Traveling Tips

Make yourself a list. I made one and it has saved me so many times from forgetting the small stuff. Sunglasses, mini laundry detergent, medications, chapstick, wallet, laptop, etc. It's amazing how much stuff I can cram into a backpack for a trip. On occasion, my jobs get extended, or I go to another job immediately without prior notice, so I have learned to pack enough clothes for a four-day job. At first, I was always over packing, and one time my suitcase literally exploded at the baggage claim. So, now I just pack for four days, and I bring the little packets of Tide you can get at Target. This way I can do laundry whenever I need to. Another great item to have is a small bottle of Febreze! Many hotel rooms just smell like ass, and older rooms that have not been renovated in some time have a musty moldy smell to them. So I would often spray some Febreeze into the intake register of the air conditioning unit, so it would go through the ducts, and allow the room to smell much nicer. You will be amazed how much this can help. I always have a large, reusable coffee cup in the side pouch of my backpack. So at night I can have a drink, and in the morning, I can fill it all the way up and have a large hot cup of coffee. The coffee cups they give you at the hotel are too small and I need a large cup! If you're a coffee drinker, you will need this too. Always pack your own mug! I would also pack a small portable Bluetooth speaker, so at night I could play some music to chill. My laptop speakers suck, so it's nice to have a small quality speaker for your tunes.

New York, NY 10-26-15

Every once in a while, with a job like House Hunters, we get the opportunity to visit a place on our bucket list. In this case, we were doing a show mostly in New Jersey, but our first day was in Brooklyn. We landed at LaGuardia around 2pm, and our hotel was about thirty minutes away in New Jersey. So Tom and I decided to take a little trip, and go see Ground Zero. I have wanted to see Ground Zero since the 9/11 attacks. The year before this, we did a road trip for a job, and drove around Manhattan. We were able to see the city from a distance, and we both wished we could have gone into the city, but our schedule did not allow it. Well, now we had that opportunity, and we both knew it would be our only chance, as after that day our job would just take us farther away from the city. Tom is a wonderful travel partner, not just because he is so easy to work with and so very pleasant to be around, but because he is also just as interested in seeing national monuments and iconic places, just like me.

We started our journey around 4pm. After checking into the hotel, and getting all of our gear in my room, we started our adventure. We asked the hotel clerk what would be the most cost-effective way to get to Ground Zero from our hotel in Jersey. He told us to walk down to the bus stop and buy a ticket into town. Transportation from New Jersey to New York City was part of the adventure! We got on the bus, and the round-trip ticket from New Jersey to the city cost $9.00 per person. Trust me, we saved a great deal considering the tolls to go from New Jersey to New York City were a lot, plus just to go under the tunnel into New York City was $14 per car! The trip was easy, even though there was lots of traffic, and it took about thirty minutes, but no hassles and very few people on the bus. We ended at the Port Authority, and then walked down several stairs and over to the train terminal. We were a bit overwhelmed, and let me tell you, even at 5pm, this place was packed with people. It's like the Atlanta airport on a Monday morning, just wall to wall people going in every direction. Most are coming home from work, or going to work, and they all take trains as you just can't park anywhere in Manhattan. The entire hub looks very similar to a large airport, and they have

Starbucks, Dunkin Donuts, clothing shops, electronics shops, and every other shop you can imagine. It's like a small outlet mall, and we had to walk several blocks underground. Tom and I followed escalators, elevators, and walkways to the underground trains, as we made our way closer to take the E train to Ground Zero. This also was an adventure as these trains were full of people going in every direction, and it's just what you see in the movies, subway trains with people offloading and loading into these underground trains.

We climbed in and took the subway to Ground Zero. This subway actually ends right at Ground Zero. When we got off, we walked up the stairs, and wow! We were right there at Ground Zero! We were two blocks away from where it all happened. This was so powerful to me and so many emotions went through my body.

I have written about other locations I have been to because of my career that had a historical impact, like Aurora or Baltimore, but Ground Zero? This was truly the most historical of any place I had ever laid feet to ground. This was the exact location of the worst terror attack ever done to the United States of America. The Twin Towers, representing financial strength, growth, and the prosperity of American economy, were destroyed by the foreign hatred of our dream. The sad truth is some other countries hate the United States. They hate us for our religion, and they hate us for our belief of freedom. So, we were attacked. They hijacked planes, and forced innocent people to their deaths, by using the planes as missiles to strike the towers. Over three thousand innocent people died that day, and hundreds more over the years just from breathing in the debris.

Yes, these were my thoughts. This is a little hard for me to write, in the sense that for the younger generation, many of my readers will not really understand the point I am hoping to make. I guess it's kind of like reading about Pearl Harbor when you were never a part of that era. I know that for them, it's just another historical timeline, but for me, it seemed so powerful and tragically sad. This was the reason I always wanted to come here to pay my respects.

When we got there, you could see all of the construction still going on for the new amphitheater, but most importantly, you could see the new tower. There were arrows directing you to the museum, and the direction to the new beautiful ponds. These were amazing. Two ponds exactly where the original towers sat, with the names of everyone who had perished surrounding each pond, etched into granite stone.

Then we walked the museum. Ground Zero Museum is an amazing display of artifacts and information from that tragic day. It takes about two hours to go through the museum, but if you had all day, you could spend it there. I highly recommend this trip to anyone who has the time to take it. September 11th should never be forgotten, and hopefully we will never see any tragedy of that magnitude again.

We were going through the museum pretty quickly as we only had a couple hours of daylight left. Once we got back out on the street, I totally wanted to grab a slice of proper New York pie! I told Tom we must find a pizza place close by before we get back on the train, and we did right down the way. It's like being in Boston and not grabbing some fresh lobster! I must say, however, this slice of pizza really sucked! I wasn't expecting that for sure, but the Ground Zero tour was worth the crappy pizza.

To make the trip even better, our House Hunters couple was so much fun. They were looking for a vacation home in an area called Greenwood Lakes. It is a beautiful nine-mile long lake surrounded by homes. Greenwood Lakes is a hidden treasure of a community, and the house they purchased was very cozy, and overlooked the lake. I really enjoyed this shoot, and was glad Tom and I were finally able to see Manhattan.

Another interesting thing about this shoot…

172

We flew into Hartford for the second part of this trip, and stayed at the same hotel from the first part of the shoot. While unloading the car, I noticed the house across the street. It was a rustic old colonial home, with a huge barn to the left, and a decaying barn to the right of the house. Obviously, at one time, this was a working farm, but now it looked liked a horror story set with a very large house in the middle. This was not just a normal house, it was a very large home, with 5,000 square feet at a minimum. Still beautiful, even though it was worn down. Two stories, six windows across upstairs and four downstairs, plus the front door. Overhang front porch, and four columns at the front steps.

Really wonderful looking home, if it was not literally right next to the highway, and right across the street from our hotel. So when I would look out my window, I would look at this amazing fifty-acre property with this massive barn. Massive like you could park a jet liner in it, yet decaying and obviously no longer in any kind of operation. The silo attached to the barn had a banner attached to it to promote a local business. I'm just assuming this brought in a little money each month to the homeowner, who now had to sit and watch all this highway traffic drive past his once successful farm.

What made this so powerful for me is that both times I stayed at this hotel, watching this beautiful property across the street, I would see the single two windows at the bottom left floor of the house lit up. There was an old man sitting in his chair watching TV, which you could only tell by the second lit window flashing a soft blue light randomly. So, I could see these two windows to the left of the front door, while the entire home was dark. The entire upstairs had no windows lit. No rooms with lights on, no rooms even lit for any reason. Both times I stayed at this hotel, it was exactly the same thing. That one room to the left of the front door. That old man sitting in a chair, watching TV, and the rest of this huge house empty and dark. One can only come to their own conclusion. To me, it was likely a single, lonely man, who had probably lost his wife years ago, and had already raised his kids, who were now married and living in other towns or states. Now, he was just existing in this huge, dark, empty home, with a farm that was now a fossil of what used to be a thriving business.

It was sad but moving. The new technology was now racing past his front window every night, yet he still had his routine of sitting in his recliner, watching his TV shows, and eating his dinner. He will, I'm sure, continue this routine by himself until he no longer wakes up, and then his legacy will retire. I can only hope his legacy was family oriented, and will be fondly remembered, and that this property will be sold and recreated into something just as happy and memorable to a future family. This entire story is just me waxing philosophically, but that's what artists do, and sometimes it's kind of fun. Kind of like an artist painting a landscape without an ending.

When Not To Be An Idiot!

Tampa, FL To Kansas City, MO 12-10-15

Tom and I had been on a long stretch of jobs, and had been in several cities and states over the month of November, and I had booked a week-long Emeril Lagasse job right before this set of jobs. I thought I was going to have some much-needed time off to regroup and relax, and then I got a text from Chris Buck, my House Hunters employer. "Emergency! One of our shooters has had a family emergency, and cannot make the shoot tomorrow in Panama City! Can you replace him?"

Holy cow! First off, Panama City is like six hours away, and the shoot starts tomorrow, I'm not even unpacked, and honestly, I'm exhausted. But Chris is awesome, and I knew this was a last-minute situation. I called Tom, and he said he would be willing to make the drive to the Panhandle, so we texted Chris and said we would cover the job.

Since the job was in Florida, and I knew parts of Panama City were a bit rough, I packed one of my pistols in my backpack. I have a Concealed Weapons Permit in the state of Florida, so this is not uncommon for me when shooting shows in Florida. We met the homeowners the next day, and had a great shoot. The show was a single mom with her two kids, buying her first home since her divorce, and it was a very compelling show. We drove back home after the last night of filming, and I got home around 1am, had a glass of wine, unpacked, and went to sleep.

Suzie and I had a busy couple of days while I was off, before I was scheduled to go to Kansas City. and then straight to Baltimore for two more shows. Our washer had quit on us, so I had the repairman show up first thing in the morning, we did our grocery shopping, some Christmas shopping, and had the home alarm guy come fix some stuff. Then, we drove our RV back from Bradenton to Tampa, because my time was up at the storage place I was keeping it, and I wanted to have it closer to me so I could work on it when I had time off.

Chris dropped off the camera and lighting gear at my house, and Tom met me the next morning so we could load up and make the flight to Kansas City.

…Are you guys figuring out what did not happen??......

Tom and I loaded up the gear and drove to the airport. We checked in the gear and then drove his car to the long-term express parking off campus. We always park in economy parking off-campus, because it is cheaper for long-term parking. We take a shuttle back to the airport, and then take the train to the airport check in. I am TSA Pre-Check, so it expedites our wait time, and we do not have to remove our shoes or take our computers out of our backpacks.

This day was like any other checking in. I was hungry, because I had not eaten any breakfast, and figured I would just grab a sandwich while we were waiting, as I have done a hundred times before. Tom and I walked through the TSA Pre-Check line, and placed our bags into the scanner. I walked through the metal detector, and waited on the other side for my bags to come through. It's not uncommon for the scanners to look at the camera bag, and then want to open it up and make sure it's just a camera. Sometimes the open Tom's bag, as he has batteries and sometimes leaves a candle in his bag, so we are used to being held back a bit just so we are good, and the TSA officials know what we are bringing on the plane is safe.

Well, that day was a little different from the norm. The roller track stopped on a bag, and the TSA official looked at the screen, and then spoke into his walkie-talkie. I was thinking, "well this is not usually what happens." Nobody said anything, and I was saying to Tom, "Well, they should at least let the other bags go through so we can make our plane. What's up?" Then they pulled the bags behind ours, and had those people go through another check line. I was thinking, "Tom, is your candle going to hold us up again?"

The metal detector guy recognized us from previous flights, and said, "Hey, you're the camera guy from House Hunters?" I was like, "Uh… Yeah, what's going on?" He said, "Have either of you been to the range lately?" I was like, "No, why?" He stated, "Well, usually this type of action is because they have found a gun."

My mind started thinking about my gun collection. I have a small .380 I keep in my girlfriends nightstand for when I am out of town, and I have a Glock in my nightstand for when I am in town, but I could not think of any reason why I would have a gun. So I was saying to the scanner guy, "I have no idea." Then it hit me! OMG! I never took the Walther out of my backpack from Panama

City! Holy Crap! I just brought a loaded firearm into the Tampa airport, right in the middle of a huge national safety crisis! What the hell was I thinking? Or NOT?

If any of you are old enough to remember the comedian Sam Kinison, he had a bit about his ex-girlfriend packing a loaded .38 in his suitcase at the airport. It was a very funny bit. That day was not as funny. Let me tell you, I was scared! I knew I had totally messed up, and I was so worried about what would happen. Not just making my flight, but making the job, or even worse, going to jail.

The Tampa Airport Police showed up, as well as the TSA officials, and some other men with badges. I knew this was not a small matter, and I was really just trying to figure out how to handle this. All of them were very calm and professional. I was assuming I would be handcuffed and taken to a small room, with big overhead lights and a gloomy table. I was waiting for a third-degree inquisition. Truth is, none of that happened. I know I am a good citizen, I have never been arrested, and I have a concealed weapons permit. I was calm and respectful, and humble to the situation. I have learned over the years by working with law enforcement, that the best way to deal with a situation is to not be a jerk.

They asked me to sit in a chair that was enclosed with simple binder ropes, just like what they use to set up the lines for the check in lanes. They took my backpack, and removed my wallet and the firearm, and started to process the situation. It actually was interesting to watch, since I had nothing else to do but wonder when the cavity search would start. You would think that area would have filled up with armed guards and officers everywhere, but it was very controlled and very professional. They knew I wasn't going anywhere, and they had total control of the situation. I was just the bonehead who actually brought a loaded gun to the Tampa International Airport. They knew I was an idiot, and clearly, they were no longer worried about me being a threat to anyone other than myself.

Tom was wonderful as usual, and he knew I was upset with myself, so he took the camera with him, just in case I was not going to make the gig. He gave me his car keys, in case they cleared me, and allowed me to put the gun back into his car in the parking lot. Then he started to find out when the next flight to Kansas City would be, so if I missed this flight, which was very probable, then I could make the next flight out.

The police were running my driver's license, as well as my concealed permit, while the TSA were running God knows what else, to confirm that I was just a normal person with a gun. Everything came back clean, of course, so one of the police officers finally came over to me and asked, "So what's going on?" Fair question, and I told him I had made a huge mistake. I was just tired from traveling, overwhelmed, and forget about the pistol. What else could I say? I told him I had a couple of days off between trips, I had the gun in my backpack, which I had forgotten about. I had not removed it yet, because at one point, I thought my girlfriend and I might be able to go to the range in those short two days together. Clearly, that was never an option, based on the amount of stuff I had to deal with once I got home, so I just totally forgot about the gun in my backpack.

All of the checkouts came back clear, so I was assuming the immediate concern was over, and the TSA official came over to confirm my phone number and address. Then they became extremely helpful, actually. A Tampa Airport Police officer came over and asked when my flight was supposed to leave. I told him, and he said, "Well, we might just be able to get you on." Since I was parked in economy parking off site, he was able to get permission to drive me in his police car to the garage to secure the weapon personally. So, we walked through the back corridor to his car outside, and drove to the economy garage, up to the fifth floor where Tom's car was. He let me put the gun into Tom's glove box, and lock it.

Then we jumped back into his police car and drove back to the airport checkpoint, and walked straight to the TSA checkpoint where I again went through the metal detector, where all of the security guards obviously recognized me. They made the standard statements, "Make sure you don't have any keys, cell phone, or guns," which I immediately failed again because I forgot to take my phone and keys out of my pocket. As all of the security guards were now laughing hysterically at me for being so dumb, they let me go through a second time, after placing those items in a dish.

The police officer that was so awesome to drive me to the garage, secure my gun, and get me back, was waiting on the other side of TSA to make sure I made my gate. His partner accompanied us to the gate, and while they were announcing my name over the intercom as a last-minute board, the three of us walked up to the gate. Myself, and two Tampa police officers telling the gate official to let me on based on a police escort. I sat next to Tom, and we both revelled in the fact that I actually made the flight.

You would think this story was over, but not quite yet. The other thing I found out, is in a situation like this, the air-crew is informed as well. So while I was the very last person to board the plane, the crew apparently all knew as well that I was the idiot who tried to board the plane with a loaded firearm. So, they were very aware as I was walking down the aisle, getting stink eyes from many of the passengers, that I was the reason their flight was delayed. The flight went fine, and at the end of the day, we made our destination to Kansas City, and I am just hoping that my TSA evaluation will go as smoothly. But we shall find out.

Just a side note during the writing of this book. I found out that my TSA Pre-Check was revoked for a period of three years, and I was charged $1500 in penalty fees. I no longer keep a gun in my backpack, as common-sense dictates. This entire situation was not good, and I was not sure how it would end up. But it ended ok, and at least I knew I would have a great story to add to my book!

Boston, MA 7-18-16

Tom and I were sent to Boston to shoot a House Hunters, and we checked into a hotel that had been booked by Chris, as always. When we check in, I usually ask for a first-floor room, so I can load our gear in and out quickly. The hotel clerk told me they did have a first-floor room available, and they booked Tom on the 5th floor. He likes to be away from elevators and ice machines, because they make noise, and as a sound guy, he hears everything. So, we always try to get him a room that will allow him to sleep well.

We drove the car around the parking lot close to my room, and I noticed my room had a sliding glass door. So I thought, "Wow, this is great! I can load and unload every day through the sliding glass door! How cool is that?" The reason this is important to me is we have so much expensive gear we travel with, and I will remove most of it when we get to the hotel, but for convenience, I will usually leave the lights and tripod in the car. So having a sliding door right by the car was great. When I opened the door to my room, I was less than pleased. I am really not a prude at all, and I have stayed in some less than desirable places during travel, and this was one. It was just dirty and run down, but what the heck, it's a hotel. Plus, I was on the first floor, so I could get gear to the car quickly.

I have stayed in shabby hotels in the past, it's just part of traveling, right? Well, not so much! My neighbor, who was two doors down, I was convinced was a prostitute! Next to her, I think was a drug dealer. Most of the nights I was there, I was trying to determine whether the cars parking next to mine were either drug deals or sex deals. It's funny how alert you become as you are seeing headlights pull up next to your car, spend about twenty minutes, and then get in their car and leave. Thirty minutes later another car, another twenty minutes, and they leave. Hey, it's a living, but not a great first night in my hotel.

The reason I believed the girl next door was a prostitute, was because of the number of men that would come to her room. When we would get back to the hotel in the evening, I would see her she just walking around the parking lot looking down at her phone. I am assuming she was setting up her next client on Craigslist, or whatever app they use for that these days. She had bright red hair, and wore the same clothes every day, but would change into a nicer outfit, and wait in the parking lot every time a John would show up. Then twenty minutes or so later, the John would leave, and she would be back in the parking lot back in her same old clothes and slippers, setting up her next deal, which would show up a bit later.

While this was going on, a car would show up to the next room down, and five minutes later that car would leave, which happened over and over again. I did notice one night, the guy staying two doors down was outside his room with a small brown paper bag, which he handed into a car that had pulled up. And then, it would all go again and again. I usually go to bed around 9:30 pm, so I have no idea what happened during the night.

One night however, I do remember lying in bed after talking with Suzie and turning in for the night. About 20 minutes later, I saw a shadow of someone sneaking up to my sliding glass door. It was a shadow of someone wearing a baseball cap. He came right up to my window, and then left. Then, about a minute later, the shadow came up again and started pounding on my sliding glass door. I assumed it must have been one of prostitute's or the drug dealer's clients trying to find the correct room, and accidently came to my room. So, I climbed out of bed, quickly slammed opened the curtains, and yelled, "Wrong fucking room!" He was startled, and laughed at me, and then stumbled away. I would have to assume he eventually found the proper room, and was able to make the transaction without a total stranger yelling at him through a window. I went back to bed, but did not sleep a whole lot that night.

I asked Tom the next morning, "How is your room?" He replied, "It's really nice, nothing like yours. They are renovating the rooms, and must be starting from the top down." I felt it would be better for me to not change my room, as I could keep a better eye on the car if I stayed on the first floor, especially since I had a drug dealer and a hooker staying next to me, earning their income.

We shot there for six days, and all six days I stayed in this room so I could keep a close eye on our rental car. I always take the camera and the batteries to charge, as well as the expensive stuff into my room, but I also started to bring in the lights and tripod, just to be safe. Not really because of my neighbors, they were just doing what they do to keep food on their table, but I did not trust any of the patrons that were visiting.

So the last day, I made the decision to change my room. I had packed up to fly out, but then found out that we were not going to be leaving until the next day, so I asked the clerk to just give me another room on an upper floor. Since Tom had said his room was wonderful, why not get a nice room? Screw the car, and screw making sure no one was going to break in to it. I just requested that they "give me a nice room for one night." The clerk gave me a key, and when I checked in with my gear, I had a beautiful room!

It was totally updated, and even a balcony so I could see my car! With a new bed, new desk, new refrigerator, and a new TV on the wall, I could have stayed in this wonderful environment for a week. It was the same room Tom had. I just never really thought about changing my room, because I could see the rental car! Stupid me learned a lesson that day. It was all too funny, but my next location makes this story look dull.

Strange Days

Austin, Texas 7-29-2016

Okay, this is a fun story. I was shooting in Texas, and we had just flown from Boston, and were staying at a Quality Inn. We had been there for a couple of days shooting the show, and in the morning on the third day, I was bringing equipment out to the car to start our day. I had just opened my hotel door for a second trip of bringing out gear, and I noticed the hotel door had just closed. It's nice when the hotel clerk gives me a room close to the exit door, as I can park my rental car close to the exit door, either on the side of the hotel or close to the front, so I can load out the gear. In this case, my room was close to the side door of the hotel.

Anyways, I noticed the side exit door had just closed, meaning someone had just walked out as I was exiting my room. As I was walking down the hallway with camera case in tow, I noticed a fabric purse on the hallway floor, about the size of a large envelope. It was green and tan, and I picked it up and opened the flap, to look inside this small purse. Enclosed was a massive amount of cash! I mean massive to me, at least!

There had to be at least thirty or forty bills in this purse, and as I flipped through them, I noticed they were all $100 bills! The stack was at least 2 inches thick, so it was probably around five thousand dollars! At first glance, I thought they were thousand-dollar bills, but then a brief glimpse of reality kicked into my brain, and I remembered they do not print thousand dollar bills! There were also some papers folded up inside, but I did not think to scope out the information, as my mind was reeling with the fact that I had a crazy amount of cash in my hand.

I have to be honest, my very first thought was "Holy shit! I just hit the lottery!" If I just put this in my pocket, and not say a word to anyone, I could pay off my credit cards and some other bills, for sure. It wasn't enough to buy a small island, but maybe a week vacationing at a small island. I am human, and this is a very fair thought to have at first. I am also me, and so I had to get this purse to the person who had just obviously dropped it, and make sure they had the cash before they left. As I walked out the side door, Tom was already by the car to load in his sound gear, so I looked to the left, and saw the car next to us already running and ready to leave. I walked over to the car's driver side door, and looked inside. It was a middle-aged woman, who was getting ready to put the car in gear and drive away. She saw me standing out of her window and as she noticed that I was holding her purse in front of my chest, her face went from confused to HOLY SHIT!

She opened the door, and thanked me for finding her. She said she was very overwhelmed that morning, and was not in her right mind, and that I was an angel for giving her back her purse. She looked disoriented, and did reach in to give me a thank you bill, but I told her I did not want the reward, and to be more careful with this amount of money.

She drove away and my mind was still quite off, trying to accept that I had just held a bunch of cash in my hands. Always a nice way to wake up, but why would someone at a cheap hotel like ours have this kind of cash? I felt really good about what I had done, and Tom and I talked about it all the way to the job site. I told everyone at the job about my morning, and the crazy incident I had gone through, and everyone said I probably racked up about a million good karma points. I wanted to buy a lottery ticket that evening after work, but Walmart does not sell tickets, so I just did my shopping and went back to the hotel. When Tom and I pulled up to the hotel, there was a car in the parking lot, and two people were getting out. It was the lady I had gave the money back to, and a man I had not seen before.

What made this strange was as Tom and I got out of our car, I looked at her and said, "Oh, hello! There you are!" I guess I was expecting to get a huge hello, and a thank you, again. Instead, I was greeted with an embarrassed look from her, and a very uncomfortable look from the man. She looked at me and said, "Oh, don't say anything, I will get in trouble," and then she giggled like she was high on drugs, and turned away. Of course, this made the man look at me like I might have been hitting on her or something, and he gave me an angry face. His normal look was similar to the look you would get when you just accidentally backed your car over a biker's motorcycle, so his angry look was even more intimidating.

I have been around the block enough times in the past, and knew the best thing to do was just ignore them both at that point. Tom and I started unloading the gear as they went inside the hotel. This seemed strange to me right away, because I was thinking, "Why am I not being praised for finding your money, and giving it back to you?" But they both just went inside as we were unloading the gear. Tom looked at me and said, " I thought that whole thing smelled like trouble." As usual, he was right.

Eventually, the man came out to his car and looked at me directly, and asked, "How much money did she drop?" So I am guessing that after our run-in she told him what happened, he came back out to talk to me. I told him, "I don't know, I did not count it, but it was a large amount. I'm just glad it was me that found it, as opposed to most people that would have kept it." He agreed, and then told me he had been "locked up for bullshit charges," and just got out! I knew immediately that this was a crazy situation, and these were bad people. She seemed drugged out, he was a convict, and the car had a paper license plate, like a new car.

If I had foresight, I would have asked myself if I keep the money from these bad people, and pay my bills to support my family, would that be ok? The answer is no of course. Since they were bad people, if I had kept the cash, and they had found out, I can only assume I would have wound up in several trash bags and dumped in a river. So, I knew I made the right choice. But what a kick in the ass to find all of this money, and do the right thing, only to find out that the right thing was to return it to a couple of crooks in a cheap hotel, probably for bail money.

That night I was talking to Suzie, and gave her the license plate number, so I did not look so obvious. After I got off the phone, I decided to walk around the corner and get a photo of the car, in case I heard on the news the next day that they just killed a busload of orphans or had robbed a bank. The sky was having a wonderful display of heat lightning, and as I was trying to take a picture of the car, the flash was not working correctly. The camera on my phone was going crazy and flash nuts, right as they were walking out of the door, of course. Why is it that whenever you are trying to do anything secret with your camera phone, it never works correctly? So now I have the crazy bitch, and her criminal boyfriend who wants to kill me, walking out the door right as my cell phone is flashing light all across their car so I can get a picture.

Yeah, just my good karma luck! The only way I saved myself from certain death was that I said the sky was exploding with heat lighting and I was trying to take pictures. Thank Heavens for God! This time, He most certainly answered my prayers. They got in their car and drove off. The next morning the car was gone, and Tom and I got on a plane to go home! Never to be seen again by these two crazy criminals.

The hopeful part of my nature would be to think that after this crazy situation, the criminal found Jesus and became a pastor at the local church, and is now helping to raise orphan children. The realist in me says he is probably back in prison.

Payback Flatulence!

Okay, in my field of work we will occasionally get producers who are not very kind to their crew. Maybe it's because they are so self-absorbed in their own world, or it's because they just feel they are better than the rest of the crew, because they are the producers. Occasionally we all have to work with these types of producers, so we work hard, try to give them the best shots, and we do our best to make them happy. You can't change their colors.

I was scheduled to shoot a show with this type of producer, and on the first day, after we all showed up, and our production assistant was sent out to get coffee and craft service. Craft service is snacks and water to get everyone through the day, so they can keep their energy up. This could be some chocolates, chips, peanuts, bananas, crackers, etc. Well, this producer had a simple list, and when the PA got back all she had was a green pepper, a yellow pepper, and a tub of hummus. We all looked at the producer a little strange, expecting something else, and her response was "I like to eat healthy on my shoots, and I know my crew is disappointed, but I don't care!"

Well, we now knew that our producer couldn't give two shits about what we wanted to get through the day, and it was all about her. So we continued and shot through the day.

Unfortunately for me, the combination of yellow peppers and hummus started a chain reaction of gas that could have stopped a small locomotive. As I was shooting the basement, while walking up the stairs I decided to "let one out", thinking that it would all be left in the deep dark depths of the basement, and eventually fade away.

Well, not so much. The shit smell stayed with my pants as I walked across the kitchen, living room, and most of the family room. It's funny how a really strong, rancid fart can stay with you for a really long time. Pretty much everyone in the house smelled this horrible gas. Most importantly, our producer was trapped in a corner by the basement door and away from any easy escape route, so she was in the fart path. She asked the PA to turn on the bathroom fan, and asked if something might be wrong with the plumbing. The smell did eventually clear out, but I am so happy knowing that it was my ass that made her so uncomfortable for a brief period of time, just like she made all of her crew uncomfortable that morning. I know it's petty, but when you feel treated poorly just because of someone's ego, it's kind of fun to do something as harmless as a good 'ole fart!

While on the topic of fart stories, it's only proper to tell them all, of course. Tom and I have worked so many wonderful shows together, and during our vast compilation of episodes, there have been many wonderful moments when we were forced to be tucked together in tight quarters for the perfect shot. This usually meant we had to climb into a shower/bathtub, so we could shoot the homebuyers walking into the bathroom or closet, and get this amazing shot of them looking in amazement at the room.

This creative shot would usually require Tom and I to climb into a tight environment, and shoot outward to capture their faces as they walked into the room. Unfortunately for Tom, that meant that he would have to crouch down by my ass, and I would stand up straight to get the shot, so he would not show up in the bathroom mirror. Tight quarters mean tight shots so we can hide from the mirrors. Poor Tom knew this was going to be a bad deal for him, as for some reason, whenever I was forced to be in a small space, my body would feel the need to pass gas. Not sure why, it was just one of those things you can't explain, like the X-Files.

So, my buddy Tom has had to endure more noxious fumes than most mortal men. Every time we were stuck in a bathroom or closet, I would light it up like the fart of July. He would have to crouch there, and consume my toxic gas, poor bastard. How he never screamed in agony during a shoot, I will never know. It was just as bad when we would be walking across a living room or kitchen, and I could no longer hold it anymore after lunch, and would just let it go, hoping no one would notice. The home buyers were in front of me on camera, but poor Tom was behind me trying to capture audio with his boom mic, while still trying to breathe, and giving me horrible looks of pain and discomfort. He was the most amazing trooper, and I'll love him forever! The best soundman is one who can accept your farts, and still love you. Cheers, Tom.

Lost Items

Okay, so I am a blond, and I represent every aspect of what a true blond should be. I have left my cell phone, keys, wallet, and so many other things all around me. I have had to go back to homes after we have all left to retrieve so many things. It's just who I am. Usually I find them quickly, but sometimes not so much. I left a small bag of cell phone chargers and computer cables in a rental car one time. They were all in a black zipper pouch, and the interior of the car was black. I filed the missing claims report and, of course, nothing was found. This was even harder to track because we were in several different states, using several different rental car companies, so it was tough just to try and figure out which rental car I left it in. To make this story short, I never found that bag of cables and chargers. I'm sure by now, it has been removed by the rental car company's lost and found, and now some young employee is charging his phone with my stuff.

Once, we were flying home from a long trip, and I was sitting in the back of the plane. A young boy behind me started to have some panic issues. I knew he was having trouble, because he was placing his finger against his carotid artery in his neck, and telling the flight attendant he was having a problem. This turned out to be a pretty significant situation, as they wound up taking him to the back of the plane by the bathrooms, and sitting him down.

When we landed, the paramedics were called. I have never seen this before in all of my times traveling, but they brought in a very small wheelchair that could fit between the seats, and they strapped him up and pulled him away, before anyone was allowed to get off the plane. I'm not sure to this day if he was having a cardiac issue or a panic issue, but I was spending my time with him trying to calm him down, and talk to him until the paramedics could arrive. With this entire issue going on, when we finally were able to leave the plane, I forgot that I had placed my iPad in the seat pocket, and left without it. I never even realized that I had left it there, until I was home and started to unpack my stuff.

This is a crappy situation to begin with, but let me tell you, when you leave an item on a plane, good luck getting it back. Lost and found is useless. It's all phone recorded messages, and when you get a live person, they are useless. You know your item is there, they know your item is there, but to actually get it before the plane leaves is like walking on water. Some things are just never going to happen, and retrieving my iPad may be one of them.

Or so I thought, and the story gets better. Good karma is something I have always believed in, and strived to keep on my side. I learned early on during this debacle, that Southwest Airline's lost and found department has no phone number. I'm sure this is to keep them from being inundated with hundreds of phone calls each day from pissed off blond travelers. I felt, however, that my iPad was very easily recognizable, because it was not only encased in a black OtterBox hard shell case, but also had a Tile stuck on the back of it. A Tile is a small square device, which in theory allows you to locate the item anywhere via Bluetooth. If the tile winds up being anywhere there is a Bluetooth signal, then Tile will send you an email telling you exactly were the device is. Southwest lost and found apparently does not have a Wi-Fi signal or phones. Uuurrgh!

I had a couple of strikes against me already, I had turned the iPad into Airplane mode, which I learned in this mode keeps the find my phone feature from working! I was also not sure how much power was left on the iPad, or how long it would stay in standby mode. I would get on my laptop every day and try to locate the iPad through the Tile app, but with no progress. I also resubmitted my lost and found claim at Southwest to extend the claim, and was very descriptive about the device.

About a month after the incident, I get a phone call from Southwest telling me they found my iPad. It was in a black Otter box case and was left at the exact terminal we had landed at! Holy cow! What are the chances? I had to set up a Fed-Ex account, and they shipped the device to me. When it came in I was so excited, but surprised at how bad the Fed-Ex box looked. It was all smashed up in one corner, and looked pretty tattered. I opened the box and again was somewhat surprised to see no packing or bubble wrap, just the iPad bouncing all around in the box. I pulled it out and at first glance could tell this was definitely NOT my iPad! It was an older model and was of course password protected. The only plus was it was connected to Facetime, so the front screen would show incoming calls.

I knew I could just reformat the iPad and keep it, but again, karma is a bitch, so I started my investigative process by taking photos of the incoming calls on my cell phone, as they only last a short time after power up. The first call was from Emma Doss, with no other info. I looked her up on Facebook, and there was one located in Texas, so I sent her a private message. Eventually, a reminder popped up for a 9am meeting with some location information, as well as some info about the meeting. I fired up my laptop, and Googled the location and info. A condo complex popped up in Texas. So, I called the number, and spoke with a lady about the iPad and some of the caller names that had come up right after I first powered it up.

She was not familiar with Emma Doss but said she would ask around, so I left her my number. Then I did a little more research, and found another number based on the meeting info I had found, and called that number. This turned out to be the attorney's office that represented the project, and they also were not familiar with the name, but said they would ask around, and again I left my number. At that point, I felt like I had done about as much as I could. Within an hour of all of this, my cell phone rang, and I answered, "Hello, this is Sean." The person on the line said, "Hello, Sean. My name is Dylan Doss, my wife is Emma, and I believe you have my iPad?" NO WAY!!!

Dylan explained to me that he had left it on the plane going back to Texas, and never even filed a claim because he just didn't feel it was worth the stress, based on the age of the iPad! So, I boxed it up and sent it to him. Dylan was very grateful and wrote a really nice thank you letter, and even sent a small gift card for my troubles. Karma points? Check!

One would think that's the end of the story, but about three months later, I received a call from Southwest saying they had my iPad! This time, I told them to please describe it, because of the mix-up the last time. She did, and was also able to get into the device to verify my info. It was MY IPAD! Thank you sweet, baby Jesus! So, they sent it back to me, and I still have it. Moral to this story, don't be a blond and leave your stuff on a plane! It's a real trick to try and ever get it back, or in my case, you just might get two of them back!

Bed Bugs

When you travel as much as I do, you're going to stay in so many different hotel rooms. It's almost inevitable that one day, you will receive the loving gift of the bed bug. I felt fortunate after so many years of traveling that I had never received this, but fortune has a funny side, and one night this devilish monster consumed me!

First off, this little bastard is super small, like a pepper sprinkle or a small speck. They grow a bit after consuming your blood, then they are a bit more noticeable, but still so small. Apparently, their feces smell similar to mold, and since many of our low cost hotels rooms smell of mold, I have never thought twice about it.

But this night would be different. I was apparently molested by several of these loving creatures during my sleep. I was bitten under my thighs, around my ankles, and all over my shoulder as I slept, yet never felt a sting. These little fuckers were eating me alive, and I never felt so much as a tickle. The next day though, I definitely knew, as I woke up itching. I looked in the mirror, and yelled, "Holy crap!" I looked like I had been attacked by a six-foot mosquito with a really bad attitude, or something of that nature. I actually first thought I had been bitten by a nest of baby spiders, but as the day progressed, I watched the welts get bigger and bigger, about the size of a half dollar. So I Googled it, and found out I had been eaten by bed bugs!

On the way to the location, I had to stop at Walgreens and get some anti-itch spray, and I pretty much used all of it just to get through the day! Trust me, you will know when you get bed bugs, because nothing itches more! I learned that AfterBite is the best product on the market to help relieve the insane itch. We shot for several days at this venue, and every minute of this I felt the itch all over my body. My only saving grace was that even though I had been bitten all over my legs and thighs, the little bastards never bit my testicles, thank God! I told Chris that night about it, and he called the front desk to complain, but they didn't care, as it was only a $75 a night room. I did change rooms, of course, for the rest of the shoot, but it took about 5 days for the welts and itching to finally go away. Don't worry, I will not include a picture of my welt-ridden thighs in this book! LOL! If I can offer any guidance to keep you from going through this while staying in a hotel room, first look at the bottom seams of the sheets for little black dots, and smell for mold. If both of these are noticed, change rooms!

Shooting in the Fall

Floral Park, NY 10-16-16

I have shot in New York a couple of times in the past for House Hunters, but I had never shot in Floral Park. Floral Park is a lovely community that is right at the entrance of the peninsula of Long Island, New York. If you ever get a chance to visit this wonderful community during the fall, I highly recommend it. What a great experience, and the colors are fantastic! The food is amazing, and the homes are all built based on the memories of our youth. The homes have red brick exteriors with fireplaces, steps up to the front door, and corner lots, with kids playing in the streets, and big oak trees. Everything you can imagine, this is Floral Park. No concerns about crazy people stealing your kids off the street, there are families all working together for soccer games, football games, PTA meetings, etc. The holidays show all the homes lit up with lights, pumpkins, decorations, and such. All the homes have wood floors, beautiful entrance ways, basements, and small kitchens that smell of wonderful food, like your grandma's house. Your best childhood memories of your time at your grandma's house during the holidays would be Floral Park. I do love shooting in the fall. All I can say is if you do get into this business, and have the opportunity to travel and shoot during this time, then you are very blessed. Please take advantage of this season, and take a lot of pictures. Not just for yourself, but for your family and friends to see what you have seen. What a wonderful opportunity to see God's gift, and show it.

The Traveling Penis
12-19-16
Okay, so after being on the road for many years with the same person, you tend to get a little humorous and have fun. Tom is my road partner. He is an amazing sound

technician, and has become not just a friend, but also a family member to me. Tom is an amazing person, and he is very smart and financially responsible on many levels. He checks the stock market and reads financial websites. He reads USA Today every morning with his coffee; he is a big reader. He is kind and soft spoken, and friendly to everyone. He is concerned about people's feelings, even people that he does not know, and he drives like an old man (very slowly). Suzie calls Tom my road wife, because he keeps tabs on my wallet, sunglasses, and cell phone that I frequently leave at airports and restaurants. All of the homeowners that we work with, as well as the producers, love him, and so do I. However, when you have a partner like this, you need to be able to ruffle his feathers a bit when you can.

One day, I was cleaning out one of the closets upstairs in my house, and found a box that had a bunch of gag gifts in it. These gifts came from friends from different parties over the years, and one of them was a dildo. This dildo was brand new in the box, and quite impressive. As I was placing it in the trash bag with all of the other stuff I was throwing away, a little deviant voice came into my mind. The voice told me…This needs to go into Tom's suitcase while he is traveling through the airport. OMG! Can you imagine his face if his case goes through the TSA scanners with a big fat dildo in it?

My better, kinder voice told me… No, that's just not right, and he might be really embarrassed. So, after talking to Suzie about it, we decided the best thing to do would be to support Tom and his kind ways… AFTER he was totally embarrassed, and that we need to put that big fat dildo in his suitcase, any way we can. Suzie even drew a face on it, and added a Santa hat, as it was close to Christmas, so a festive dildo was much more appropriate. Luckily, a couple of weeks later, Chris had us scheduled on a couple of jobs back to back with tight flying schedules. So, I recommended to Tom that he stay with us overnight between flights, as he has done in the past.

Tom and I had driven across the state from one job, and we had to fly out very early the next day. So when we got home, we had a glass of wine with dinner, played with the puppies a little, and then watched some TV. After that, Tom went upstairs, and went to bed. This gave me the perfect opportunity to place that dildo into his suitcase! Suzie helped me, of course, as she loves him as much as I do. The next day, we headed off to the airport in the early morning.

To make this story short, but as funny as it should be, he made it through TSA checkpoint with no worries. Even though you know they saw it in the scanner, and I'm sure they took a picture of the screen, just like they did when I had a handgun in my backpack! When he retrieved his bag and then opened it up to place his car keys inside, he saw a big fat dildo pop out at him, and he bent over in laughter and tears. It was one of my best days ever!

Every time Tom opened his bag to retrieve his iPad or headphones during the flight, he had to look at, and hide, this massive toy of joy! I sat directly across from him on the plane, and I think we were both crying the entire flight! Even the stewardess was wondering what was wrong with us? Tears of joy for sure. The next task would be disposing of this without looking like a creepy creepster when we got to the hotel, but I left that task up to Tom. My job was to call Suzie, and tell her what a success our little scheme had been.

I considered making him our travel companion for fun, and calling him Waldo, from Where's Waldo?. Fortunately for all of us, we decided against this. LOL

Albany, New York. Winter Storm Stella 3-14-17

This was a second trip for a House Hunters episode. We had already shot the first part of this show, and the weather had been beautiful! Seventy degrees, green grass, and wonderful locations. We were scheduled to shoot the scenic's for this episode during the first leg of the trip, just because that's how they scheduled it. So we did shoot some wonderful shots, and then went home waiting for the second leg of this trip.

A couple of weeks later we were scheduled to finish the show. Before we even left Tampa, we were aware that a pretty bad snowstorm might be hitting Albany. So we were packing warm clothes to prepare us for the weather, but we were never prepared for what this storm would bring!

It was called Winter Storm Stella and the night we landed, it was supposed to start around 4am. I'm not a weather guy, and I wasn't really paying much attention to the upcoming storm, so when Tom and I landed we did our normal routine. We picked up our rental car, went to Walmart, picked up some food and wine, and then headed to the hotel. Tom and I got to the hotel and checked in, and I then did my usual routine of calling my Suzie and my son, and then plugging in the battery charger to get the camera batteries all topped off. I put everything together for the first shoot day, and then went outside to have a quick smoke. The weather seemed fine! I even took a picture from my cell phone showing the hotel parking lot with no snow on the ground, and relatively decent weather and clear skies.

Winter Storm Stella was going to be a combination of two weather systems converging during the early hours, and eventually becoming one major storm. The two storms converging is called a bomb genesis. This is a two-part process, first the storm has to move out over the ocean, and then the center of the storm quickly becomes more intense. Meteorologists call this type of storm system a weather bomb!

As the storm strengthens, wind and precipitation spikes. It happens when atmospheric pressure nosedives over a short period of time, meaning this average snowstorm could morph into one with hurricane force winds. This happens because the two storms converge and become one perfect storm! Yes, just like the movie, this storm was created from two different storms merging into one. We had a cold weather storm crossing the top portion of the United States, as another storm was heading up the east coast, mixing into the top storm creating major winds, as well as major snow.

I was only learning this from the Weather Channel, as I got into my room to realize that everyone on TV was saying tomorrow would suck for us. It was kind of hard to believe because as of that time, the weather was fine with no snow. Maybe everyone was wrong, and this would just pass through Albany, and we would just have some wind or flurries. I watched the Weather Channel all night, as opposed to my normal Investigation Discovery or Forensic Files programs. Eventually I went to sleep, and just assumed we would be fine.

As I get older, I have learned that us old people now have a new sleep pattern, that means we get up at 2 or 3 o'clock to pee! Around 2-ish, I woke up and relieved myself, as I usually do at the ripe old age of 48. After my early morning relief, I looked out the window to see a beautiful visual of our rental car starting to gather some snow on it. Not a crazy amount, but about an inch or two. The snow was falling pretty heavy, so I knew the Weather Channel was probably correct, and I would just have to see how the morning would be.

I woke up in the morning to my phone alarm, and immediately looked out the window to see an amazing sight! Our rental car, as well as every other car in the hotel parking lot, was covered with snow! Literally covered, with probably a good foot at least! After a quick shower and some coffee, I trudged out of the hotel through the snow, and loaded up our gear. Tom met me wrapped in winter clothes, and we started to clear off the windshield, and made the drive to the location. The roads were empty, and full of snow and ice. It was a slow drive to the location, and visibility was very poor. The first thing we found out was that the homeowners were still at the house, and even more interesting, was that they would be there all day with us!

Usually when we do a home tour for the show, the realtor schedules the home, and tells the homeowners to leave for the day, so we can shoot the show. I had never shot a home tour with the homeowners still in the house, because that would make our job very difficult. As we are moving from room to room shooting a tour, you don't want to accidentally get them in the shot, sitting on the couch watching TV. That day there was a good reason for them to be home, as the Mayor of Albany had declared a state of emergency. Which meant no one was to leave or drive, all schools were closed, and all curb parking was towable by the city, so they could get the snow movers through the streets! This obviously made all parts of our show more difficult, to say the least!

Our Production Assistant never showed up, of course, as driving conditions made most sane people stay at home. We had to trudge through the snow just to get our gear up to the house. Of course, this home had a long row of steps up to the front door, a long row of snow-and-ice-covered steps. First, I got the camera out of the car to try to get it acclimated to the weather, without it freezing up. Our producer Brian showed up, and we all just agreed that we would have to work around the family being home with us, as there was just nothing we could do. To make it more interesting, they had pets, dogs and a cat that were running through the house all day.

Tom and I unloaded the car of gear, and carefully got everything up and into the house, without slipping on the ice-covered steps. Then we started the show. First was the walk up, when the realtor and the homebuyers walk up to the house. Brian, our producer, had left to move his car to try to get a parking place where he would not be towed. Much later, as we were prepping gear and getting ready, we realized we had not heard from Brian in over a half hour. He finally called, and said he had moved the car, but could not get back up the hill to the house! He was stuck a block down the road at a gas station, and that we should just start shooting the walk up without him, as he was starting the slow, snow-covered walk back to the house.

Tom and I had shot this show for years, so that was not a concern, but getting our producer back to the location in a blizzard was becoming a concern. We shot the walk up without Brian, but the most difficult part of this sequence was the fact that snow flurries were constantly falling onto the camera lens. I had a lens rag with me, and was wiping the lens every couple of seconds, but I was concerned none of this footage was going to be usable, because of the water that would pool on the lens glass after wiping it so frequently. We just shot it and hoped it would work out. Brian did eventually get through the snow, and we did continue the show, but our bigger concern was how we would ever get out of this location. The snow kept coming down, and the weather was not getting any better!

As the day went on, we shot our scenes, and worked around the pets and the family as best we could, and just made the best of it. At lunchtime, we were trying to figure out what to do about food. We did not have a PA to go pick up anything, and clearly, we could not drive anywhere, as our cars were now covered in three feet of snow. So we decided to try and walk down to the gas station at the end of the road where Brian had parked, as they had some food. Brian had noticed that when he was trying to park his car down there. We trudged down through the snow, and made it to the gas station, where they did have a small deli with some sandwiches we could microwave, so we could have a warm lunch. It was actually quite tasty, and they also had warm soup, so we had a nice gas station lunch. Then we trudged back up the icy hill to get back up to the house, as the snow was still falling down like rain.

When we finished the day, our main concern was how the hell were we going to be able to leave? Since the cars were covered with snow, we were afraid we would actually have to spend the night in these poor people's home. They didn't want that, and we didn't want that, we just want to get back to our hotel and relax. The cars were engulfed in snow, literally all the way up to the rearview mirrors. We used a shovel to dig and dig and dig, and finally got our cars mobile. Then Brian said, "Hey, can you guys follow me to my hotel? Because it is up on a hill and I want to make sure I can get into the parking garage with this ice." We did follow him to his hotel, and boy, he was right. The hill up to the parking garage was insane, and totally coated with ice. I had to literally climb behind his car and push, as he floored the gas pedal, to get his car up the hill. Eventually, the car behind us was willing to also push from his bumper to get Brian's car into the parking garage.

This was most definitely a crazy storm, but we made it work, and we got home every night, safe and sound. The story came out great, even with the silly weather. Talk about an adventure! Not only did we survive Winter Storm Stella, we made a great show during the "Perfect Storm".

Tweak Your Space 2015

While I was returning from shooting a bunch of House Hunters shows, I received a call from someone I had never met before. Her name was Debbie Perez, and she had been recommended to call me because I was working with House Hunters, one of her favorite shows. Debbie has a unique decorating business, and was considering making a TV pilot to pitch to HGTV. Debbie owns a business called TweakyourSpace ,and her talent is repurposing existing items that are already in the home. She works with a crew that help her with moving furniture, hanging light fixtures and pictures, painting walls, etc.

Debbie has a great eye! She's able to go around someone's home, and not only move the furniture around to make a space look larger and more inviting, she would also go out to the garage or shed, and find things to add to the room to make it pop. The premise for her business came about when the economy was so poor. Instead of starting from scratch with all new furniture and accessories, spending thousands of dollars to redecorate a room, why not hire Debbie to dig through all of your existing stuff to give you a new look? It was a cool premise for a show!

We started shooting some of her client's homes, while she was working on them. We wanted to get some B-roll and cool shots of her work. We shot several different homes, and captured some crazy things. A couple of my favorites were a chandelier falling from a two-story ceiling, and when one of her workers accidently knocked over an aquarium full of crickets.

The chandelier was supposed to be carefully removed, so it would remain in one piece. We were up on scaffolding, but unfortunately when her crew undid the supporting bolt, down it went into a bunch of pieces. I was able to shoot the entire crash, and Debbie's reaction was "Well, that was not supposed to happen." It was great, and reminded me of a skit from the British show Only Fools and Horses. Between the chandelier catastrophe and the crickets, this made for great filming, especially watching them wrangle the crickets back into the cage. Of course, we captured some amazing transformations! I really was hoping this show would take off. Debbie is very talented at what she does, and the show seems to be a good fit for an HGTV or DIY network. Unfortunately, again, I've learned how hard it is to get any show in front of a network. At the end of the day, so many agencies are pitching so many shows. It seems, if you're not on the inside, you will probably not get a show to air. I am still hopeful that the show gets sold, as Debbie is a blast to work with, and very talented. It would be a great opportunity to stay local and be home with Suzie and the dogs each night, as opposed to having to continue to travel so much. Fingers crossed.

Antiques Roadshow
4-11-17

In April of 2017, one of my friends called me with a show opportunity. He was really busy with other work at the time, and just did not have time to take on another project, so he asked me if I would like to work on a show called Antiques Roadshow. I had watched this show for years and really enjoyed it, so of course, I wanted to be a part of the experience. I called the production coordinator and she requested that I put together a crew for a three-day shoot in Sarasota at the Ringling Art Museum. The premise of this show is that it's basically a traveling road show, and at each location or venue, the local residents bring in any antique or interesting items they have at the house. Local antiquities curators will explain what the item is, its monetary value, and any significance it may have for free. Tons of people show up for this event. The Ringling Art Museum is a gorgeous facility and this really made a great venue for such an interesting show.

I called a good friend of mine, David Cook, who is one of the best gaffers in town, and he assembled a crew for us. Since the show was going to be in Sarasota, which is about an hour and a half from the town where Dave and I live, we stayed at my mom's house in Bradenton. She and her husband, Bob, were out of town on a cruise, so it worked out perfectly. Dave and his girlfriend, Brora, stayed with me during the show, so we would not have to drive so long every day. What a blast! Antiques Roadshow schedules a specific amount of venues per season, and then travels to each venue for a week to set up, and then record the show. They have camera crews outside and inside the venue, filming the appraisers as they look at the items people bring in. When an item is of specific interest, production coordinators will radio to the producers about the item. If they feel it would make for good TV, then they move those people from outside to inside to discuss the item with another appraiser on camera, and this is done for the full three days. Then all of these shots are edited together to create the hour-long show we all love to watch. I never really thought about how this show was put together in the past, so it was really interesting to see. I worked directly with the lighting coordinator on this show, so I had an inside look at the entire production.

It is the same as when you watch the Mecum Auto Auction, or anything similar. Just a whole lot of product and dialogue shot, and then the best and most interesting ones are put together to make the show. A production like this has so many working parts and elements to it, and I cannot even imagine how they started the show so many years ago. Now, it is cookie cutter to them, and they know exactly what parts to use to create a very fluent and interesting show. The traveling production crew for Antiques Roadshow was great, and so very appreciative of the job Dave and our crew did. It is really nice when an out of town crew gives you praise for your hard work, as they work with local crews in so many towns, and we were blessed with "You guys are one of the best crews we have ever worked with!" It was hugs, handshakes, and a big smile driving home from this show.

Fantastic Food
9-16-18

After so many years of being on the road, I made a decision this last year to stay home more, and not travel so much. I had to say goodbye to House Hunters, as the only way I could work on that show would be to travel out of state for many weeks at a time, and I wanted to be closer to my family. I started reconnecting with the local crews, and was able to get some local jobs as they came along. One in particular that I felt was worth writing about, was a show that the First Unit guys hired me for. It was a Travel Channel cooking show called Fantastic Food.

It was only a couple of days, one in Daytona, and the next day in Orlando. The premise of the show is similar to Emeril's Florida, as we meet local restaurant owners and showcase their food and signature dishes. The first day was in Daytona Beach at a nice little place called the Daytona Tap Room. It was large in size, allowing many people to dine. They were having a reggae band play that evening, so we could not only film the environment and the food, but also show that they have live music as well.

When I showed up in the morning, I realized that the best way to unload my van was in the back alley, because I could go back in and unload all of the gear to set up. This worked out great, since the bar was in the very back of a long building with several other bars and restaurants. So I backed all the way to the rear of the establishment, and dropped the ramp to roll out my equipment, and set up all of the lighting gear inside the restaurant using the back door.

We shot for many hours, highlighting different food dishes and filming interviews, and the day was going along pretty much without a hitch, until the band showed up. They also backed their trailer into the alley to unload the drums and guitars and music equipment. I mentioned to the owner that at the end of the night I would need to be able to drive out of the alleyway, and they would have to move their truck, as it was clearly blocking me in. His response was "Oh yeah, no worries. They will move when you need them too."

So, we continued to shoot, and as usual, as the night progressed, the production crew wanted to shoot more and more stuff. By that time, they were pretty much wrapped, but only five minutes from their hotel, so why not just keep shooting the action, and all of the people drinking and having a great time? To be honest, I was looking at my watch, because I knew after we wrapped, I had a long drive back to Clearwater. Then the band started to play. They were a local reggae band and they were really good. I love Reggae, but I started to get concerned, because I had a four-hour drive home that night, and it was already 10pm, and I really wanted to get on the road. The director finally said, "That's a wrap." So I started to fold up the light stands and load the van. I realized as I was bringing gear out to the van, that the band's truck and trailer were still blocking me, and now they were on stage playing. Crap! So, I went inside and found the manager, and told him I had to get on the road as quickly as I could, because of the distance I still had to travel to get home.

His response was "Well, they are playing now. So you are going to have to wait until their set is done, and then ask them to move the truck!" I waited for another hour for them to finish their set, and then had to lean over to the drummer to tell him that they had to move their truck, so I could get out. He was like, "Oh, okay, dude. Just let us finish this last song and then we will move it." So, they did another song, and once I was able to get a bunch of stoned reggae players off of the stage to move the truck, we then found out that five other cars were now parked in the alleyway in front of them! We had to go into each bar and find the drivers, and then get them one by one to move all of their cars, so the band's truck could pull out, so I could drive out. By this time the entire crew had left well over hour earlier, and was back at the hotel.

By the end of the night, it all worked out, and I was able to get out of the alley and back on the road about 1 am. But lesson learned on this gig: Don't leave your gear van in the alley when a ton of other cars are going to block you in. They are there to drink and party, but you just want to get home after a long day. Never listen to the day staff when they tell you they will get you out when you need to leave. I should have just moved the van after unloading it, and parked it across the street. No harm, no foul, just a long night but great reggae! I had those songs stuck in my head all night during the drive home.

Docomo Koji Mochinaga
3-20-19

Yeah, you try and pronounce that name!

One Monday morning I was lying in bed having my coffee, and trying to wake up, knowing my schedule for the week was not full of work. I had no work scheduled, so

I did what I usually do on Monday mornings, and I sent out group texts to both the local rental houses, as well as my production friends, letting them all know I was available if they needed any help with upcoming work. I have mentioned First Unit many times, but since retiring from House Hunters, Sunwolf Lighting and Grip has also become a huge help for me. Greg Wolf started his own rental house several years ago, and he is awesome to work with. I do this pretty much every Monday morning if my calendar is slim, just as a way to get a job or two. This has always been a good practice for me, as it has landed me more work than you would believe, because the persistent worker gets the work, and I have never been afraid to ask for a gig! Out of sight is out of mind in this industry, and it never hurts to let the local production companies know you are available.

Rick from First Unit sent me a text ten minutes later, telling me that my timing was impeccable and asking if I would be available for a three-day shoot at IMG. Yes! Of course, and so I was booked, and glad I had reached out. I received a call from Doug a couple of days later about the job at IMG Academy in Bradenton, Florida. IMG Academy is a sports training facility, that offers specific instruction on many different sports. The Academy specializes in one on one, as well as classroom training, for younger and older students with great skills in their sports trade. IMG Academy houses some of the best coaches around as instructors for our young and upcoming amazing athletes. Doug told me this was going to be a huge job, with a lot of crew and three truckloads of equipment! The client was to be a superstar tennis player named Docomo from Japan, and we only had a couple of hours to shoot his interviews and scenes, but we had two days to set up, and then the day to shoot, tear down, and then load out.

I have worked on several jobs over the years like this. Tiger Woods was one I did many years ago, and it was the same deal. Set up for days, and then be ready for him to come in and promote his endorsements for an hour or two, and then he will leave.

Superstar personalities have this type of schedule, and you just deal with it. You have them for a very specific time frame, and then they have to go to the next venue. This is just the way it is, and our job is to be ready for them. Lord knows, the director does not want to have to wait on lighting or camera once a high-profile personality shows up.

For this gig we had to do something I have never done before, and to be honest, I was really excited to be a part of this gig. With the First Unit jobs, I'm normally just a grip or a crew load in/load out. As a DP/ Camera guy, I have a passion for the visual arts, but even though on this job I was a grip, I was really interested in what we would be doing with so much stuff. It's funny that in this industry, regardless of whatever your position is, you love all aspects of it, and it's so fun to see big projects and everything involved, as they are put together.

What made this job so exciting was the fact that we were going to surround a tennis court with twenty feet high green screens all the way around the court. Three hundred and sixty degrees of green! Has this ever been done? Twenty feet high, three hundred and sixty degrees around the court! How friggin' cool is that? This was insane! And we did it by placing twenty-foot high, twelve-foot wide green screens hanging from pipes, and slowly raising the poles as we added more green fabric. We had placed clamps and pulleys from the ceiling to hold the weight, so they would slowly raise the poles and the green screen, one by one until they were all set in place. We would pull on ropes, all at the same time, to raise the poles from the ceiling pulleys, and then we placed boards between the end seams of the green screen with clamps, to smooth out the ends.

This made the fabric look like one crazy long sea of green. It is kind of like taping sheets of paper together to make one long sheet, without seeing the ends of the paper.

Once the roughly five thousand square feet of green screen fabric was surrounding the tennis court, and we had the entire perimeter enclosed, we then started lighting this mammoth set. Any lights inside the set had to be covered with green screen fabric around the large silver light stands, and we also placed several very large lights on Super Crank stands on the back side of the set, that would allow the lights to be raised high enough to get over the 20 foot high green screen, and then point them towards the inside of the set. All of this had to have cable run to the lights to power them, and that as well had to be covered in green fabric, in case it ended up in the camera shot. After this was set, another crew came in and placed a Matrix style camera setup to capture him in an amazing jump shot! They had 67 Canon DSLR cameras wired together across a curved rail around the rear of the set. A Red digital 4K camera was at each end of the rail to capture the video at the start and end of the sequence. This was basically a 280 degree broken circle with all of the cameras placed around the track, which was then also covered with green screen fabric.

As Docomo jumped from the ground to return a ball to someone off camera, the 67 cameras all went off at the same time. And when all of those images, including the video cameras, were processed through the computer, we had an amazing image of him jumping up in the air, and then a 280 degree turn of him in still motion spinning around before he came back down! Really impressive, and such a wonderful project to be a part of, so I could see how this was actually done! The final shot looked exactly like The Matrix!

This was only one of four other sets that had to be created in this venue for Docomo to be a part of, but the green screen set alone had a crew of seven, including me. After the day was over, we had to remove everything and load it back into the trucks, and turn the tennis court facility back into a normal useful environment, as we do with every other venue we shoot at. It's not uncommon for jobs like this to have long hours, especially the final day, because you have to wrap everything you spent two or three days to set up. I think we wrapped the last night around 3 am, but I was so wired after watching all of the cool shots that had been done that day, it just inspired me to always be creative and passionate about my craft. How great is it that after all of these years, and all of these experiences I have been blessed to be a part of, I am still just as jazzed about it as I was when I first started my career, so many years ago! I truly am blessed.

Vice President Mike Pence
3-28-19

In the middle of March, Bill Mills called me and asked if I was available to work with him on an interview in Naples. It would be with the Vice President of the United States, Mike Pence. Mike Pence is the former Governor of Indiana, and was nominated to the position of Vice President by our current Commander and Chief, President Donald J. Trump. I was available, and honestly excited about this gig, as I am personally a Trump supporter, and this would be the first time in my career that I would have the opportunity to work with such a political dignitary. I checked my schedule, and I was available, so I agreed to work with Bill on this. I had to send all of my personal information to the Secret Service, who would be running a detailed background on me to make sure I was okay to even be in the room with the Vice President of the United States.

I was happy to provide my information, as in the past I cannot tell you how many federal background checks I had to go through while working on COPS. Plus, I recently renewed my concealed weapons permit without any issues, and was not immediately handcuffed and taken to some dark dungeon, so I knew all would be fine as expected.

Once the background check had cleared, I started to get the coolest emails ever. They were labeled from the White House, Office of the Vice President, and they were his itinerary for the day. One after the other, I started to get these White House emails every day, even after the shoot, and it was so very cool. I did notice that within about a week or so, all of these emails had been removed, not by me, but I am guessing by the White House. I do wish I had printed a couple just to have them for prosperity. To this day, I cannot retrieve a single White House email from my computer.

For the shoot, we would be at the Ave Maria University, located just East of Naples. The Ave Maria University is basically its own town in the lower middle of central Florida, with a community of homes, shops, and of course, a very large church. This community was also the home of the Mother Teresa Museum, and this building is where the Vice President and one of the news anchors for the Catholic Church news organization, EWTN, would have an on-camera conversation about his views on religion and abortion.

The morning started out very early for me, with a 3:30am wake up to take a shower and drive to Bill's, who lives about an hour south of me. Bill wanted to be on the road by 5am so we would have plenty of time to get to the location, unload our gear, and go through the Secret Service security check. The security check was fun to watch, as we had to open every gear case and lay it on the ground so the bomb dogs could sniff the gear, and then a crew of security specialists went through the gear by hand to evaluate and make sure we did not have anything that could be conceived as a weapon. We, of course, went through the metal scanner and were then wanded to make sure we also did not have any weapons on us. Thank God I made sure this time I did not have a gun in my backpack. I'm a blond, but not that much of an idiot, at least not twice!

After reading the itinerary, a couple of things came to my attention pretty quickly. The first was the minimal amount of time we would get to pre-light the interview. The next was that after the one hour we were given to light the set, we would have to remove all of the equipment and hide it in a large closet. The reason for this was that after Vice President Pence gave his speech, he would be given a tour at the Mother Teresa Museum, and they did not want our equipment all over the room. So, we were given the hour to get an idea of how the set should be lit, then had to remove all of the gear during his tour, and then re-light the set while he was doing meet and greets down the hall. Then he would come back into the lit museum, and have his on-camera dialogue with the news anchor.

The crew consisted of Bill Mills, myself, Bill Mumford, and a sound guy from Miami named Mac McNamee. Mac was a nice guy, and he had clearly done presidential interviews in the past, as he was very aware and understanding of the process. We rolled the gear into the museum, and started to set everything up. Time was critical, so once we were told by the producer where the interview would take place, everyone knew what needed to be done, and we worked very efficiently. This was the first time in my career that I was setting up gear while being surrounded by Secret Service agents. The entire hour was used setting up the gear and cameras, and framing anyone who was willing to stand in place so we could look at our placement and lighting. When we felt we had it set up, our producer came in, and said, "Great! Now put everything in the closet, you have 20 minutes!"

Normally, this would be a crazy thing to hear in my industry, but when you are surrounded by Secret Service agents with guns, and interviewing the Vice President of the United States, it sounded pretty understandable. I did realize how obvious it would be to tell the Secret Service agents from the rest of the crowd, as they all wore the same outfit: blue slacks, blue overcoat, and an American flag lapel pin, as well as the curly lead coming out of the back of their neck and going into their ear. It was also pretty obvious due to the fact that in Florida during the warm weather of March, you don't need to where a thick fabric blue sports jacket, unless you have a small fully automatic weapon hanging by your hip.

We did just that, loaded all of our lights, cameras, and gear into a closet, and pulled all of the extension cords, and placed everything in that closet. I was allowed to place very small strips of yellow tape on the floor to mark where all of our light stands and tripods had been, so we could at least remember where we had originally placed them. I also took photos on my phone, so I could remember what stand went to what yellow tape marker. Then we were led out of the museum, and to an outside waiting room to sit for two hours. Bill and I had a plan for when they allowed us back in to divide the workflow. Bill and Mumford would grab their cameras and set up a shot, and I would grab all of the lights and get them back in place, based on the photos I took on my cell phone to get everything as close as we had it. Then we would tweak until the Vice President came in, and then shoot. Talk about a time test, it was almost like being timed to set up an interview, and shoot in 20 minutes! We had a plan based on our circumstances, and we were going to make it work. The entire job could not be more out of our control, but honestly, the fun was being tasked this way.

While waiting we had a sandwich and some snacks, and we discussed how quickly we could get this set back up, while the Vice President was speaking across the building. Then, after looking at our watch realizing we were 5 minutes behind schedule, the Vice President's liaison came up to us to say, "The VP wants to shoot the interview outside!" WHAT? We are lit for an inside interview! The sun is in the wrong place, it will look awful, and the wind is horrible! Really? Bill's face dropped, and I knew his mind had just exploded! He was speechless! He told the liaison all of this, and she said she would see if she could get him to change his mind, but he was pretty adamant about shooting outside. Bill said that he would need access to the outside of the building, so he could look at it to see if we could light for it. This was something that would have to be cleared for us to even go outside. At this point, we were at the mercy of the Secret Service, but they did give us clearance to look outside, so we all left single file to the outside of the building. As we were walking outside, we passed the museum entrance right when Vice President Pence was doing his tour. So to the left of us were five military officers completely decked out with full armor, including ballistic helmets, bulletproof vests, and fully automatic machine guns hanging from them without any sports jackets! They were not hiding anything, and it was quite clear who they were, and why they were there! Of course, my first thought was "Jeez, I hope I don't drop anything and that this camera does not look like an assault rifle." These guys are the shoot first, ask questions later kind of guys, and I really did not want to end my film legacy as a tape outline on a church sidewalk.

This to me was still so incredibly awesome to see, as I want our President, Vice President, and dignitaries to be protected, and what an amazing show of force in the proper way. After looking at the outside area, it was obvious to everyone that this would never work for an interview. There was too much wind and horrible light control, so the decision was made to shoot inside, and so we had to hustle to get the lights back in, and get everything ready very quickly again. Thankfully, we had this down by then. We went back into the museum, and double timed the set up. Bill and Mumford grabbed their cameras and tripods, and set them up based on the tape marks we had left, and I grabbed every light and placed it right back into position in minutes! We set up as quickly as we could while the Vice President was doing his meet and greets. As he was coming our way, we tweaked each light, and set up our original setup as best we could. Bill had the producer, and whoever was in the room, be stand ins for camera focus. At one point, we even had a Secret Service agent act as a stand in, because we needed it. They understood, and before we knew it, the Vice President was in the room and ready to be filmed.

Once everyone was in place, and we started shooting, all went smoothly. That was the first time I had a second to look at my phone for the schedule. As the news reporter was talking to the Vice President, I was looking at the itinerary emailed to me from the White House and saw his planner for the day. I thought my schedule was tough? Our day was to arrive early to setup and shoot his interview. His schedule was to fly from DC to Naples, caravan to Ave Maria, give a speech, do meet and greets, do our interview and outside stuff, caravan back to Naples, get on Air Force Two and fly to Jacksonville, give a speech, and then fly back to DC that night for Trump's rally speech.

What the heck? How does anyone do all of that in one day? This is one guy and in one day, the Vice President not only had a full day, but also a HUGE schedule! As I would later find out, because I did continue to get the White House emails every couple of days, his schedule never let down! It was almost every day, several locations and several speeches, photo shoots, and interviews! I thought I had long days, but it sure put things in perspective. I am glad I am in production, and not politics.

I understand that at this time our political structure is so fragmented, I see every day how divided we are as a country. Republican, Democrat, or Independent, I see the hate and the anger opposing parties have toward each other, regardless of religion or position. We see the blame and the opposition on a daily basis, without a thought of how hard these elected officials work for us. It's a shame and I am sad to see it, because I love America, and I promote freedom. God Bless America. I support our people, I support our troops, and I hope this country always stays strong and "for the people." Never against them.

There have been so many other projects that did not make this book. The best part of loving what you do is all of the stories and memories that you forget along the way, because there are so many. So many friends who worked alongside you and lessons learned, as well as mistakes made during the course of life. This is what makes us who we are, and what we will become, and how we will end. This is our true life lesson, and the legacy we will leave to our young ones.

In Closing:

I have been in this business for over twenty years now, and I have loved every single moment of it. Yes, some days were very tough, and some very humbling. But I would not trade a single day for any other career. I feel so blessed to have made filmmaking my career, and I thank my God and my family for guiding me in the right direction more than the wrong. Life is a gift, and please don't ever take it for granted. Every day is precious, and you should always be learning and laughing. May you go forward with a kind heart and an amazing attitude. It will take you so far. God bless you and your family.

SMD

Acknowledgments

First and foremost, I want to thank God, our Lord, as He is the reason we all are on this planet to do all of the amazing things we do everyday.

My bride and soul mate, Suzie, who has been with me through this entire process, reading, correcting, laughing, and giving me hope and support.

My beautiful son, Kasen James, who inspires me everyday to excel. My wish is to mold him into a wonderful man, who will hopefully have his own family in the not too distant future, and will raise his children to excel, just like Daddy did with him.

My family, of course, who all have supported me and loved me regardless of the crazy job I aspired to do. Mom, Dad and everyone!

Bill Mills and Curtis Graham, who have both mentored me in this career. Both of you are so gifted at your craft, thank you.

All of my friends and workmates I have had the pleasure to spend my days with along the way. Each one of you has talent and skill beyond words.

Sean Hayden and Meghan Daigle for helping me with the technical side of self-publishing and Tony Panaccio for all of his creative guidance along the way, Madison Paige for formatting and John Allison for his amazing book cover!

About the Author

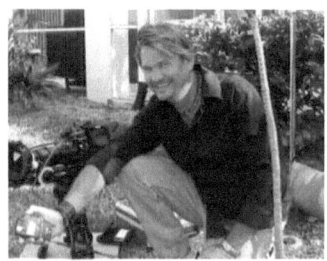

Sean Michael Davis started his passion for the entertainment industry at a young age. He was raised by two generations of broadcast industry professionals.

Sean took his talents into the trenches of true reality TV, and mastered his camera art of cinema Verite. Sean worked on COPS (FOX) for three seasons, working as a Field Producer, as well as shooting for their other show JAILED (SPIKE TV). While working on COPS, Sean started his own documentary film, Skyway Down. Sean spent about three years shooting and fine-tuning the film until its completion, and then submitted it to Sunscreen Film Festival, winning Best Florida Film (2011). Sean is the only Florida resident to win Best Florida Film twice from the Sunscreen Film Festival.

Sean has worked on feature films such as Dolphin Tale and The Punisher, filmed in Tampa and Clearwater, as well as shooting for major networks such as FOX, CBS, HGTV, The Cooking Channel, HSN, ID, National Geographic, The Weather Channel, Food Network, ESPN, USA Network, and several local networks.

For the full experience, please visit

www.shoottothrillbook.com

If you enjoyed this book, please leave comments on
Amazon.com

www.ingramcontent.com/pod-product-compliance
Lightning Source LLC
Chambersburg PA
CBHW020902180526
45163CB00007B/2592

* 9 7 8 0 5 7 8 4 9 9 9 6 3 *